RELIGION AND SOCIAL SYSTEM OF THE VĪRAŚAIVA COMMUNITY

Recent Titles in
Contributions to the Study of Anthropology

A Nilotic World: The Atuot-Speaking Peoples of the Southern Sudan
John W. Burton

Culture and Christianity: The Dialectics of Transformation
George R. Saunders, editor

The Psychodynamics of Culture: Abram Kardiner and Neo-Freudian Anthropology
William C. Manson

Pilgrimage in Latin America
N. Ross Crumrine and E. Alan Morinis, editors

The Art of Native American Basketry: A Living Legacy
Frank W. Porter III

Franz Boas, Social Activist
Marshall Hyatt

Sacred Journeys: The Anthropology of Pilgrimage
Alan Morinis, editor

RELIGION AND SOCIAL SYSTEM
OF THE
VĪRAŚAIVA COMMUNITY

DAN A. CHEKKI

Contributions to the Study of Anthropology,
Number 8

GREENWOOD PRESS
Westport, Connecticut • London

Library of Congress Cataloging-in-Publication Data

Chekki, Danesh A.
 Religion and social system of the Vīraśaiva community / Dan A.
Chekki.
  p. cm.—(Contributions to the study of anthropology, ISSN
0890–9377; no. 8)
 Includes bibliographical references and index.
 ISBN 0–313–30251–0 (alk. paper)
 1. Lingayats. 2. Lingayats—Social aspects. I. Title,
II. Series.
BL1281.24.C54 1997
294.5′513—DC21   96–29950

British Library Cataloguing in Publication Data is available.

Library of Congress Catalog Card Number: 96–29950
ISBN: 0–313–30251–0
ISSN: 0890–9377

First published in 1997

Greenwood Press, 88 Post Road West, Westport, CT 06881
An imprint of Greenwood Publishing Group, Inc.

Printed in the United States of America

The paper used in this book complies with the
Permanent Paper Standard issued by the National
Information Standards Organization (Z39.48–1984).

10 9 8 7 6 5 4 3 2 1

Copyright Acknowledgments

The author and the publisher gratefully acknowledge permission to use the following:

Extracts from *Vacanas of Basavanna*, by L.M.A. Menezes and S. M. Angadi (Trans.). 1967. Edited
by H. Deveerappa. Sirigere, India: Annana Balaga. Reprinted with permission of Sri Taralabalu
Jagadguru.

Extracts from *Sri Channabasaveshvara: Life and Philosophy* by R. C. Hiremath. 1978. Dharwar,
India: Karnatak University. Reprinted with permission of Karnatak University.

Extracts from *Śūnyasampādane* by S. C. Nandimath, L.M.A. Menezes, and R. C. Hiremath (Trans.).
1965–1972, 5 vols. Dharwar, India: Karnatak University. Reprinted with permission of Karnatak
University.

Dedicated
to the memory of

Shri. V. C. YAGATI

*who made a significant
contribution to the
Vīraśaiva Studies*

CONTENTS

ILLUSTRATIONS

Figures

Table

PREFACE

In the modern global economy and mass society there is an urgent need to understand the intricate relationship between the material and spiritual values. The increasing rate of change poses some bewildering and complex problems for modern societies. Community leaders and legislators are frequently confronted with public debates and controversies on a wide spectrum of social problems that have some relevance to religion and morals. Among young people and quasi-religious movements, the winds of change are blowing.

Despite all the modern scientific and technological advances and relative affluence, we are unable to live in peace and harmony. Although the cosmic religious experience has been the strongest and noblest mainspring of scientific research, the individual in a technological mass society becomes an atomized, depersonalized, alienated being influenced and controlled by material objects and large complex organizations.

Pitirim Sorokin identified a cyclical process of sensate, ideational, and idealistic cultures. Albert Einstein remarked that "science without religion is lame, and religion without science is blind." Sigmund Freud emphasized the deeply emotional basis of the human religious urge. Emile Durkheim suggested that religion arises out of the experience of living in social groups; religious beliefs and practices affirm a person's place in society, give people confidence, and enhance feelings of community. Max Weber embarked upon a broad comparative study of the relations between religion and society.

In contemporary post-industrial societies, however, religion, god, morals ,and spiritual culture seem superfluous.The rapid growth of science and technology, materialism, and the process of secularization, it is believed, will inevitably lead to the weakening, if not the extinction, of religion. However, recent events and processes around the world seem to contradict this notion. In a complex, materialistic, fast changing society there is now, more than ever, a great need to maintain a balance between the religious and scientific views of life.

Science is unable to tell us how to improve human personality and behavior or how to reconstruct more humane societies. Science is more helpful with our means than our ends. Religion, however, plays an important role in formulating some of the criteria for moral judgement in defining our goals. Religion helps us comprehend reality from different perspectives and makes some sense of coherence and meaning in the world.

Religion takes many forms and plays different roles. It can be a solid foundation for the social cohesiveness of a society, or it can be a powerful source of tension and conflict. The experience of misfortune, inequality, injustice, suffering, and death give rise to profound questions. Religious beliefs and symbols provide a context of meaning by which these experiences can be dealt with when other forms of explanation and problem solution have failed. Religion helps us to struggle with evil and resist greed, lust, and hatred. It strengthens moral fiber and encourages us to strive toward conflict resolution, humane relationships, and peace. In other words, religion should be the binding force that deepens the solidarity of human society.

The indifference, if not contempt, that many persons have for religions other than their own has been a source of prejudice, discrimination, tension, and conflict, primarily because of ignorance or lack of adequate knowledge of different world religions. All religions, as Albert Schweitzer observed, are bound together in a holy partnership to advance the cause of peace, justice, and freedom. A study of other religions is essential for the understanding of one's own. Studies in comparative religion indicate not only the perplexing variety of religious beliefs and practices, but also many common elements characteristic of different religious systems. Today we can learn more and draw inspiration from more than just one of the existing religions. This book, hopefully, will serve this purpose.

This book is intended to be neither theoretically oriented nor encyclopedic in its content. There is unavoidable repetition in a book of this kind. I have made no serious effort to avoid this, partly because it would have impaired the thematic autonomy of each chapter, and because recapitulation and reiteration of the fundamental religious principles in different contexts have relevance and value in themselves. However, I do believe that there is a certain unity of approach that binds the different chapters. This book is intended for students of religion, society, and culture, as well as for the educated public interested in the comparative study of religion and the social system.

ACKNOWLEDGMENTS

The interdisciplinary nature and complexity of this study can hardly be underestimated. It was necessary to rely on a variety of pertinent sources in medieval and contemporary Vīraśaiva religion, philosophy, and literature. My indebtedness to these sources, as listed in the references, is gratefully acknowledged.

The chapters on ethics, psychology, theology, and philosophy of Vīraśaivism were originally written by my father, Shri. V. C. Yagati (1900-1976). These essays served as a major source and appear in a revised form in this book. He received degrees in both philosophy and law from the University of Bombay, and published several essays and books on religion, philosophy, and literature during the 1919-1975 period. He was one of the pioneers in disseminating the Vīraśaiva religious literature to the English speaking world. His article on Basava was published (1928) in *The Indian Social Reformer*. He prepared an English version of the Vīraśaiva classic, *Shoonya Sampādane*; a major portion of this work was published in the 1940s. In the early 1950s, he completed the task of rendering into English more than nine hundred Vacanas, or gospels of Basava. His book on *Society, Religion and Culture* (in Kannada) includes many of his seminal essays. In view of his significant contributions to the Vīraśaiva studies, this book is dedicated to his memory.

I would like to express my sincere thanks to Dr. Terrence Day, Professor of Religion, University of Manitoba; Dr. George Kurian, Professor of Sociology, and Dr. Raj P. Gandhi, Professor of Sociology, of the University of Calgary; and Dr. John Badertscher, Professor of Religious Studies, University of Winnipeg, for reading this manuscript at various stages of its development. Their incisive comments enabled me to improve the manuscript in many ways. Of course, I alone am responsible for any inadvertent errors or misinterpretations.

My profound gratitude to Laureen Narfason for her diligent editorial assistance. George Hamilton deserves much thanks for bibliographic assistance. His special interest in this study, his friendship and sense of humor helped me keep up my spirits. I am grateful to Lesley Murphy for her patience and efficiency in preparing this manuscript for publication. Lynn Taylor and Jim Sabin at Greenwood Press have guided me through the publication process. Finally, I wish to thank my family: wife Sheela, and our sons, Mahantesh and Chenaviresh, for their love and affection that enabled me to complete this project.

PRONUNCIATION

The pronunciation of vowels is approximately as follows: a lengthening sign as in "ā" indicates a long vowel; "e" and "o" are always long; "r" should be pronounced similar to the "ri" in ring or river. The following remarks apply to consonants: "c" should be pronounced as in church; "j" as in joy; "ś" similar to "sh" in ship; "h" after a consonant as the "th" in hothouse.

RELIGION AND SOCIAL SYSTEM OF THE VĪRAŚAIVA COMMUNITY

Part I

THE PATTERNS
OF RELIGIOUS CULTURE

1

VĪRAŚAIVISM: A PROLOGUE

Among the several religious communities of India, Vīraśaivism, and its followers, known as Liṅgāyats, manifest unique characteristics. The Vīraśaiva community in India has an estimated population of more than 10 million. The Liṅgāyats numerically constitute a major community, and they play an important role in the socioeconomic and political life of the state of Karnatak. They also form a significant minority in North America. However, the Vīraśaiva religious and social structure, as an object of Western academic interest, has seldom received adequate serious scholarly attention. The Vīraśaiva religion constitutes a unified system of beliefs and practices that unite into one single moral community (Durkheim, 1995). The Vīraśaiva religious community (*Gemeinde*), for more than eight centuries, has been a dynamic system closely bound up with a set of cherished ideals. The system of religious values, the social structure, and the pattern of evolution of the Vīraśaiva community are intertwined.

This book is oriented toward viewing the Vīraśaiva religious tradition not as an isolated entity, but as an integrated cultural complex whose historical evolution, philosophy and ideology, social structure, and cultural dynamics have contributed toward shaping the Vīraśaiva world view (*weltanschauung*) and life-style. The Vīraśaiva culture is viewed as a context within which norms, organizational structures, and behavior patterns are examined (Geertz, 1973). The Vīraśaiva religious ideals provide a model of harmony and a synthesis of the materialistic and spiritual world views. Furthermore, this study attempts to show that the life blood of the Vīraśaiva community is its culture: the religious values and traditions, the common history, the social structure, and the shared dreams and hopes for the future. The Vīraśaiva religious norms, beliefs, and behavior have bound its followers into a dynamic moral community. Despite the fact that the Vīraśaiva community has been undergoing a process of unfolding of continuity and change over the past several centuries, it has in many ways retained its distinctive culture.

Unlike Brahmanic Hinduism, Vīraśaivism has an egalitarian ideology stressing the essential equality of all human beings, and rejecting inequality based on birth and other inherited biological traits. Max Weber (1968:19) observed that in the Middle Ages, the ancient sect of the Lingāyat represented a type of particularly sharp and principled "protestant" reaction to the Brahmans and caste order in India. It is a community where women are free to participate in various social and religious activities. Vīraśaivism permits divorce and the remarriage of widows. Women are not required to observe ritual pollution and purification rites after the menstrual period or after childbirth. Many women have made a significant contribution to the Vīraśaiva philosophy and literature.

Vīraśaivism has rejected problematic features of traditional Hinduism, such as priestly elitism, temple worship, and ritualism. The Vīraśaivas uphold monotheism, but they do not recognize the characteristic forms of the Hindu caste system and the four lifestages. The Lingāyats bury the dead and they do not observe pollution and purity rituals associated with death. Furthermore, they do not accept the authority of the Brahmanic Hindu Scriptures and extol the Kannada "sayings" of the Vīraśaiva mystics.

The Vīraśaiva work ethic does not view work purely as the means of one's livelihood, but includes a vital social goal as well. The work ethic incorporates the notion that the fruits of one's labor are to be shared with others in the community. Unlike the individual self-interest characteristic of the Protestant ethic, the Viraśaiva concept of work (Kāyaka) includes ethical principles related to community sharing and selfless service (dāsoha), diligence, thrift and sobriety. The principles of sustainable development, nonviolence, and peace form an integral part of the Vīraśaiva way of life.

Vīraśaivism emphasizes the importance of honest dedicated labor (kāyaka) as a "calling" (beruf) and makes no distinction among different kinds of occupations and professions. The members of the Lingāyat community are involved in almost all occupations, including those that are considered ritually polluting by the traditional Hindu caste system. Work is not only recognized as worship, but it also is considered as heaven itself insofar as a Vīraśaiva engaged in an occupation need not even be concerned about worship or meditation.

The members of the Lingāyat community are expected to carry on their worldly activities as a divine service. In this sense, work is not intended to be a means of acquiring wealth. Excess gains beyond one's means are not meant for savings, investment, production, and accumulation of capital, but should be shared with those members of the community who are in need. This inevitably gives everyday activity a moral and religious significance.

Commitment to community, selfless service, sharing (dāsoha), monotheism, egalitarianism, dedicated work (kāyaka), acquisition of righteous knowledge, nonviolence and peace, freedom, rationalism, humanism, a righteous code of conduct, and a frugal life-style are the fundamental Vīraśaiva values characteristic of this little-known religious community. In other words, the Vīraśaiva ideology embodies the ingredients of a humanistic democratic universal religion.

The Lingāyats constitute a distinct community by virtue of sharing a set of common beliefs, customs, symbols, and rituals, values, and behavior patterns. They have a rich spiritual-cultural heritage. This community, comprised of networks of organizations and institutions, is held together not only by bonds of religion and culture, but also by ties of kinship and social interaction (*Gemeinschaft*). A strong sense of belonging, moral interdependence, mutual obligations, and a deep sense of community identity are characteristic of the members of this community.

The term "Vīraśaiva" implies "heroic" (*veera*) Śaiva because of their intense devotion towards Lord Śiva and because of their heroic attitude and behavior in defending their faith. The Vīraśaivas also are distinguished by their unique practice of wearing a prototype emblem (*Linga*) of the Lord Śiva. Hence they also are called "Lingāyats." Therefore, the terms "Vīraśaivism" and "Lingāyatism," in this study, are used synonymously despite the controversy that revolves around the origin and evolution of this community.

The origins of the Vīraśaiva religion are uncertain. The traditional school of thought claims that Vīraśaivism is of great antiquity. It is regarded as an offshoot of Śaivism, also known for its devotion to Lord Śiva. The legendary origin of Vīraśaivism takes us far back in time to when the Five Prophets (Revana, Marula, Ekorāma, Pandita, and Visweswara) founded and preached this religion in eons gone by. The scriptures composed in Sanskrit, such as "Sivāgamas" and "Siddhānt Sikhāmani," are recognized as major sources of this school. The modern school of thought (Sakhare, 1978; Ishwaran, 1992), however, argues that Basava (twelfth century) was the founder of the Lingāyat religion. The religion is distinct from Brahmanic Hinduism because it does not recognize the Vedas and repudiates the caste (*Varna*) system. This school relies on the Kannada "sayings" (*vacanas*) of the twelfth century Lingāyat saints as the main source for understanding the fundamental principles of Lingāyat religion and society. These "sayings" manifest a zeal for social reform.

This book attempts to address questions such as: What are the distinct cultural characteristics of the Vīraśaiva system? Part I is based on the original sources (in Sanskrit and Kannada) and presents an historical and comparative analysis of the religion and philosophy: the notion of God and the Guru in the Vīraśaiva religious tradition, ethics, psychology, theology, and philosophy. What are the unique features of the Vīraśaiva social structure and patterns of social and cultural change? Part II provides a sociological focus on the intricate relationship between religion and the social system. It includes an examination of the social vision of Basava, the monastic organization and social structure, the family and community, the status and roles of women, and the future of the Vīraśaiva community in North America. These chapters, delineating the sociocultural fabric, are based on my sociological studies of the Vīraśaiva community in India and in North America, spanning more than thirty-five years. Part III provides an overview of the role of foreign and indigenous scholars in the development of knowledge about the Vīraśaiva religion and social structure. It traces the beginnings of modern scholarship related to the Vīraśaiva studies from the early nineteenth century to the 1990s, evaluates trends of research on the Vīraśaiva religion and society during the past three decades, and outlines the research agenda for the twenty-first century. We begin with the following chapter by delineating the Vīraśaiva concept of Śiva, the Supreme Reality.

2

ŚIVA: THE VĪRAŚAIVA CONCEPT

In classical Hindu mythology Brahma, Vishnu, and Śiva are linked together as the gods of creation, preservation, and destruction, respectively. In the various Śaiva scriptures, however, Śiva is portrayed as the one God overall, who is ultimately responsible for creation and preservation as well as destruction.

Among the major Hindu gods, the antiquity of Śiva is shrouded in mystery. Archaeologists have identified the precursor of the God Śiva in his Pashupati form in the Indus Valley civilization that existed about 7,000 years ago. In the Vedas and Upanishads Śiva appears as Rudra, representing the untamed aspects of nature. Śiva is depicted as a great ascetic continually wrapped in meditation. He is a god of mystical stillness, but also the Lord of the Dance and the universal teacher. He is married to Pārvati, His abode is Mt. Kailās, and He uses Nandi as His vehicle and so forth. The epics and several scriptures extol Śiva and his divine powers. Among the religious schools that recognize Śiva as the supreme deity, Vīraśaivism in the Kannada-speaking region of India, is unique. This chapter is intended to present an overview of the concept of Śiva in the Vīraśaiva religious tradition.

The Vīraśaiva bhakti movement that centered on the worship of Śiva alone, and no other god, emerged in the twelfth century as a revolt against all forms of inequality and injustice. Basava and a host of other Vīraśaiva saints preached universal equality, nonviolence, dignity of work, and humanism. They practiced what they preached and attempted to create an egalitarian society.

Vīraśaivism upholds a staunch belief in the existence of the Supreme Power. God is the one only, without a second. He is Śiva the Almighty creator of this Universe. The life mission of a devotee is the ultimate merger of the individual soul with Śiva through devotion, knowledge and proper action.

Vīraśaiva saints describe Śiva as a handsome and attractive young deity, and sometimes as a benevolent and indulgent father whose kindness knows no bounds. Sister Mahādevi describes Lord Śiva:

> I adore the Handsome one:
> He is imperishable
> He is without form
> He is eternal and divine
> He is without birthmarks
> I admire Him O mother. Listen.[1]

Each saint seems to conceive the personality of Śiva according to one's liking and imagination. It seems that they do not attach importance to any particular fixed form of the deity (Nandimath, 1979). The underlying principle in Vīraśaivism, in conceiving the Supreme Being in a personal form, appears to be to approach the unknown through the known, that is, from the concrete to the abstract, from the human to the cosmic form.

Basava, the leading Vīraśaiva philosopher-poet of the twelfth century, speaks of Lord Śiva:

> Embracing form and formlessness
> Thou art the form, O God: Thou art
> Also the formlessness
> Thou art the universal eye, O God;
> Thou art the universal face, Thou art
> The arms of the universe, O Lord![2]

St. Prabhu *(Allama Prabhu)* queries: When the body itself is the temple of God, why ask for a temple? Basava believed that building temples is not necessary because the devotee's body and soul can be transformed into the Divine. He says:

> The rich build temples for Śiva
> but poor as I am
> What can I do?
> This, my body, is my temple –
> My legs are its pillars,
> My body is the sanctum
> My head is verily the golden pinnacle
> O Lord!
> Matter is perishable
> But not the spirit.[3]

In the early stages of one's spiritual life, however, a Vīraśaiva is expected to worship his or her personal *Istalinga* or Linga (prototype of Śiva Linga in temples) as Śiva. The Linga is the divine symbol par excellence. The Linga operates as a symbol at three levels: the gross, subtle, and causal. So the activities of the physical body in the conscious state, the activities of the subconscious in the subtle body, and the activities of the unconscious in the causal body are all actually activities of Linga itself. In the later stages of one's spiritual journey, according to the Vīraśaiva conception, Śiva has neither form, nor no form, but has both form and no form. In other words, Śiva has formless form. This is indescribable, invisible, unimaginable, and so forth. The Linga is at once immanent and yet supremely transcendent.

Vīraśaiva saints speak of Śiva as the glorious essence of Lustre in all Lustre. St. Prabhu says:

> Waiting for your Vision,
> I gazed:
> it was like the instantaneous dawn
> of a million million suns,
> a trillion of thunderbolts
> to my amazement.
> O Lord,
> if you are the effulgent light
> there is no metaphor.[4]

He is neither of this world, nor of the other world. They speak of Him as existence, consciousness, and bliss, the eternal and the all-pervasive.

In their mystical journey, Vīraśaiva saints slowly enter into the mystery of the Universe, attributing the mystery to Śiva. They admit the impossibility of tracing the beginning of the Supreme Deity and fathoming the depth of the Infinite. Śiva, being eternal, is beyond the state where creation, subsistence, and dissolution prevail. Śiva resides in all things and living beings. He pervades the Universe and is beyond the Universe. A Vīraśaiva mystic, St. Prabhu (*Allama Prabhu*), exclaims:

> Lord, You are found,
> On mountains, in caves and vales,
> Lord! You are found wherever one looks!
> O Sir, You are,
> Incomprehensible, invisible,
> Here and there and everywhere![5]

St. Prabhu depicts the presence of divine Immanence:

> As a spark in stone,
> As an image in water,
> As a tree in the seed,
> As silence in speech,
> So Thou in thy devotee
> O Lord[6]

Though Śiva pervades all things and is perceived in all things, for the devotees, all things are not Śiva. The Vīraśaiva saints seem to understand the final stage of their spiritual journey as beyond the power of any human beings to express and indicate, but only to be felt and experienced. At this stage they address the Supreme God Śiva not with any name, but only as Void or Space (*Bayalu* or *Śūnya*), which in the terms of Christian theology might be described as the divine ground and abyss. It is something that cannot be comprehended or seen; it is viewed as a great inexplicable Light Divine which corresponds to the Upanishadic "Absolute."

Istalinga (*Śiva Linga*) is the symbolic representation of this universe. It is the symbolic microcosm of the macrocosmic deity Śiva, and it is the object of meditation and concentration rather than that of mere formal worship. The devotee looks upon *Istalinga* (*Śiva Linga*) as his reflection, and follows a gradual course of subjective culture of the soul so as to be free from the worldly attachments, miseries, and cycles of birth and rebirth. Eventually, a devotee comes to be essentially one with Śiva, thereby merging the individual soul with the Universal Soul. It is the ultimate depersonalization of the individual soul, beyond the cycle of birth and death.

Worshipping the symbol (*kuruhu*) of Lord Śiva in the form of Istalinga, the devotee yearns to realize the divine consciousness (*aruhu*) that transcends the symbol. Vīraśaivism equates the God with the community. The notion of God in Vīraśaivism signifies a dual commitment, the commitment to the doctrine of individual liberty and equality, and an equal commitment to community and society. The Vīrasaiva concept of Śiva energy (*śakti*) and Śiva community provides a sociospiritual framework within which the devotee may enjoy individuality without losing his or her sense of community.

In sum, Vīraśaivism believes that Śiva is the author of all creation and its evolution. St. Devara Dāsimayya says:

> This earth is thy gift, its harvest, too;
> The wind that blows around us is thy gift.[7]

Śiva is the ultimate reality from which all beings are born, by which they move and live, and into which they enter after dissolution. There are thousands of devotional lyrics, composed by Vīraśaiva saints, in praise of Lord Śiva. The following lyric (Nandimath, Menezes, and Hiremath, 1965) illustrates the Vīraśaiva concept of Śiva:

> Though you can see Him,
> He has no form;
> Though you can seize Him,
> He has no body:
> Although He moves,
> He has no motion;
> Although He speaks
> He has no speech
> To those who curse Him
> He is no foe;
> To those who praise Him
> He is no friend
> Did you hope to catch
> Śiva's glory
> In a net of words,
> You must be a simpleton![8]

The complete self surrender to Śiva, by the Vīraśaiva saints, is expressed in the following:

> Thine the body, thine the mind,
> Thine all the wealth we own!
> There is not an atom here
> But what is thine![9]

The sublime state of the final union of a devotee's soul with Śiva is narrated by a Vīraśaiva mystic:

> Consciousness past consciousness;
> Unconsciousness beyond
> unconsciousness;
> And union beyond union;
> Ecstasy past ecstasy:
> That is the state
> Of unity with Śiva![10]

Basava describes Lord Śiva thus:

> He is the cause and
> essence of all souls.
> Incomprehensible,
> without beginning, middle or end,
> neither the scriptures
> nor all the sciences
> can tell about him
> this, or that –
> the great, the glorious
> Lord Śiva.[11]

> He is the one who knows.
> He is beyond knowledge,
> beyond sound.
> He is the Supreme Bliss of Ecstasy.
> He is without parts
> Lord Śiva
> is the light glowing
> from the peak mass of light,
> thousand-rayed, splendourous,
> irradiated by a billion suns.[12]

These lyrics of Vīrasaiva saints depict Śiva as a concrete, as well as an abstract, primeval energy that is conceived as the creator of the entire universe. The next chapter discusses the importance of the Guru in the Vīraśaiva religious tradition.

3

THE GURU IN THE VĪRAŚAIVA RELIGIOUS TRADITION

The concept of the Guru represents a spiritual guide and preceptor par excellence. The Guru plays a key role in the spiritual life of the Vīraśaivas. The Guru, because of his extraordinary superhuman or charismatic personality, has a unique spiritual influence on his devotees. The devotees have a special relationship with the Guru for spiritual initiation and guidance.

The devotee maintains communication with the Guru through meditation, prayers, and association. This enables the devotee to focus on the Supreme Reality. The Guru embodies all that is sacred and represents the Universal Soul. The Guru has a paramount role in the spiritual life of a devotee by providing instruction, guidance, and example. It is argued (Miller, 1976-1977:533): "The dynamic, sacred centre within Hinduism continues to be the enlightened guru whose charismatic leadership creates the institution for philosophical, religious and social change, guiding Hinduism in new directions that transcend the limitations of traditional sectarianism and that seek a dialogue with other universalist religious points of view."

Historically, the Guru has played a major role in the development of the diverse Hindu traditions. There is a common belief that the Guru is God himself. Throughout the centuries, Hindu tradition has been renewed and revitalized at times of crisis by great men and women who have had the creative genius to blend the old and the new in religion and society. Louis Renou (1963:29) observed: "Under the influence of enlightenment, a man breaks with his past, starts preaching a new doctrine and after many ordeals succeeds in gathering around himself a body of disciples from among whom shall be formed his successor. After his disappearance, his biography is shrouded with legends; here lies the great influence of a guru on the Indian mind."

The Guru occupies a distinct place in the Vīraśaiva religious tradition. The ultimate goal of a Vīraśaiva is to reach the final stage of union with God. This is accomplished by following the six-phase spiritual (Ṣaṭsthala) system. Knowledge of the self is a prerequisite for the attainment of God. So the devotee accepts a Guru who guides him in the process of spiritual progress. The Guru takes out the internal spiritual spark of the devotee and presents it to him in the form of Istalinga. The devotee worships his Istalinga, follows selfless dedicated work (*kāyaka*), and conforms to the religious and moral codes of Vīraśaivism. Finally, the devotee attains the state of union with the Supreme Reality, Śiva.

The concept of the Guru in Vīraśaivism refers to the spiritual mentor and guide who initiates the novice into the Vīraśaiva spiritual odyssey. The devotee's reverence to the Guru knows no bounds (Nandimath, 1979). The guru is the cause of the spiritual birth and hence he is regarded as both father and mother. The Guru is considered to be worthy of more reverence than is due to Śiva, the Supreme, because it is the Guru who leads the soul to unity with Śiva.

Several Vīraśaiva poets and saints, alike, have extolled the preeminent role of the Guru in achieving spiritual goals. It is through the grace of the Guru that the devotee realizes that the key to liberation is firm devotion to Śiva. In Vīraśaivism, devotion is an important factor for the realization of the self and God. The Guru's grace is also crucial for the devotee's eventual merger with God.

The harmonious relationship between the Guru and the devotee is best expressed by St. Cennabasava:

> The Guru and the disciple should be
> Like light hidden in light,
> Like an image hidden in a mirror,
> Like a pearl hidden in a crystal tube,
> Like the heart of a body's shadow,
> Like holding mirror to mirror.[13]

Vīraśaivism includes three kinds, or rather refers to three functions, of the Guru: the initiator or Dīkśa Guru, the instructor or Śikśa Guru, and the liberator or Mokśa Guru. Although these functions may be performed by the same or a different Guru, each one is revered without distinction. Moreover, the Vīraśaiva religious tradition suggests that the Guru is not only Śiva himself, but also one more powerful and influential than Śiva.

The devotee's dependence on the Guru for knowledge, experience, and, more importantly, the grace necessary for the attainment of the ultimate union with Śiva, leads to a very personal and intimate communion with one's Guru. The Vīraśaiva literature depicts face-to-face dyadic relations between the devotee and the Guru. Such dyads are symbolized by the intimate and unique relationships of father-son, mother-child, lover- beloved, and husband-wife (Ramanujan, 1973). Max Weber, the reputed German sociologist (1968:305), observed: "The Guru carried the newcomer through the steps toward full membership, the eight (*ashtavarna*) sacraments which alone gave the right to full membership." Furthermore, Weber points out that, "obedience to the Guru was strong in the Lingāyat, stronger than in any other Indian sect."

Vīraśaivism recognizes the spiritual preceptor or Master (*Guru*), a prototype symbol of God (*Linga*), and the itinerant religious mentor (*Jangama*) as the different manifestations of Lord Śiva. The Guru, as an institution as well as a concept in the Vīraśaiva religious tradition, as noted by Ishwaran (1983), refers to the distinctive ideological institutional structures. Within the conceptual complex of the Guru, Linga, and Jangama, it is significant that the concept of the Guru is assigned primacy. It is relevant to emphasize that in the Guru institutional system, while the disciple-devotee is free to choose his own Guru, the Guru is equally free to choose the disciple. Vīraśaivism tends to nourish only the kind of Guru-disciple relationship that is based on mutual understanding and respect.

It is the Guru who, in the process of Linga initiation, places the Linga symbolically on the palm of the disciple. This is not just a ritual, but one that is expected to have a profound sociopsychological impact on the devotee, leading to a metamorphosis of body and mind. St. Siddharāma was initiated in the Linga lore by St. Cennabasava. The former describes his experience:

> By Guru's grace, I forgot
> this ephemeral body.
> By Guru's grace, I purged
> the mire of the triple impurity.
> By Guru's grace and by
> The triple initiation,
> I got the Experience.
> By Guru's grace, I knew the worth
> of the Pure, the Perfect and the Absolute.
> There is no other thing
> To me greater than this.[14]

Although the Guru, Linga, and Jangama are considered as Śiva's different forms, the Vīraśaiva tradition does recognize the paramount importance and unique position of the Guru. The lyrics (*vacanas*) of Vīraśaiva saints emphasize the significance of the grace of the Guru in the spiritual life of a Vīraśaiva. St. Cennabasava stresses the unity, identity, and the supreme role of the Guru:

> The Guru is the great God,
> God is the Guru, the Guru is God.
> There is none more worthy than the Guru,
> As he is the initiator.[15]

> Once you remember the glorious feet
> Of your glorious Master,
> The bonds of birth have ceased.[16]

> When once the holy Guru has cast his form
> And been transformed to formlessness,
> There is no room for doubt.
> He in the body taught you;
> Accepting your body, he made you pure;
> Merging within your life, he made you perfect;
> Made one with Self, he made you the Supreme.[17]

Basava also indicates that the Guru is Śiva Himself; his word is holy, an alchemic stone. He also reminds us that the scriptures do declare: "greater than the Guru there is none."

St. Siddharāma also was convinced of the manifestation of God as the holy Guru who, in turn, became the Linga, sacred formula (*Mantra*), consecrated food (*Prasāda*), and Jangama. He praises the glorious Guru for liberating him here and now. St. Siddharāma also makes it clear that the Guru is he who has become the triple Linga's primal spell and who has destroyed the worldliness besmearing him, and changed from form to formlessness. Furthermore, he emphasizes the vital role of the Guru in reaching Śiva:

> O impenetrable Śiva
> Whom none can penetrate,
> My Guru has penetrated
> And brought you to my palm.[18]

Sister Muktāyi is quite aware of the significance of the Guru in the spiritual life of a Vīraśaiva when she argues that, without the Master's word, Linga, Jangama, Prasāda, and one's self cannot be known. More importantly, without the Master's grace, the final union cannot be realized.

St. Prabhu describes his experience of the sight of his Guru as follows:

> My whole being, within and without,
> Bathed in supernal splendour,
> I have gazed at the Source of all light!
> I have seen my Supreme Master
> With his gaze of unfathomable wonder
> Concentrate, beyond all emblems,
> Upon the emblem on his palm.
> And having seen, I have been saved.[19]

Although the Guru neither speaks nor listens, St. Prabhu asks Him for a word of grace and appeals for rooting out his senses' error and razing out the dullness of his mind:

> Even if you be silent without,
> Speak to me in silence within,
> I will still clasp your sacred feet.
> Should You do so, I will take Your Grace,
> But should you not, still will I take it,
> Merely by being Yourself.
> Thus, howsoever it may be,
> I will annihilate myself for You,
> And so obtain Your grace.[20]

St. Prabhu describes the lightning flash of illumination that he experienced when he encountered his guru, Animiśa, in a state of trance,

When Grace strikes, earth is turned to gold;
The common stone is charged with alchemy,
When Grace strikes,
The Bliss that years and years
I sought for, look!
Now flashes upon my sight![21]

Sister Mahādevi speaks of her esteemed Guru and holds Him in high praise, because it is the Guru who will protect those who approach Him in distress and despair.

O my Guru
My obeisance to you with gratitude
For you have liberated me
From the entanglements of my mundane life
And showed me the Life Divine.[22]

Basavalinga Śarana (Chekki, 1986) reiterates similar conceptions of a Guru when he makes a plea for the Guru's Grace.

Your spiritual sun's rays
Destroy lust;
You give us courage
In times of crisis;
Supreme Guru,
Bless me with your Grace![23]

It is important to note that the Vīraśaiva religious texts demonstrate that a devotee favored by the Guru has none equal in this world; and if the Guru blesses, even a blind person will be able to see. The Guru is the protector and kith and kin of devotees. The foregoing evidence suggests that the Guru is not only the heart of the Vīraśaiva religion and philosophy, but also a major influential force in the spiritual development of the devotee. A righteous way of life is a *sine qua non* for the achievement of spiritual goals. Let us now turn our attention toward gaining an understanding of the ethical bases of Vīraśaivism.

4

ETHICAL BASES OF VĪRAŚAIVISM

It is universally recognized that moral philosophy is the basis of all major religions in the world. A religion that has no moral basis is as shaky as a house built on sand. Moral norms influence both the material and the spiritual worlds. Moral activity is the essence of good conduct. A person is measured by his/her good intentions and proper actions. Everyone is judged good or bad insofar as our actions are conducive or harmful to the welfare of the society as a whole. The standard of morality may differ in different cultures and times but the universal principles remain the same under all circumstances. J. S. Mackenzie (1924:1), a moral philosopher, defines ethics as "The science of the ideal in conduct." Ethics, as a branch of philosophy, deals with human actions from the point of view of their rightness or wrongness as a means for the achievement of ultimate happiness. Every person acts with some ideal in view. Our ideal or goal may be happiness in this or the next world (spiritual world). To achieve this happiness, we should act so as not to come in the way of the happiness of others. In the pursuit of the public good, the good of the individual is inseparably involved. The Vīraśaiva poet, Sarvajna, elucidates this principle in his saying, "Whoever regards others as his own self attains final bliss."

In the twelfth century of the Christian era and in the following centuries, there have been a number of Vīraśaiva mystic saints whose contributions to moral thought and action have been significant. Their exquisite thoughts and high moral characters induce us to follow them in their footsteps. These saints (*śaranas*) are distinguished by their rationalistic way of thinking, and their eradicating of sheer dogmas and superstitious beliefs from religion. If we try to understand the Vīraśaiva mystics and their speculations on the Vīraśaiva philosophical system, we realize the height of moral and spiritual progress they had reached. They pursued the ideal, not with a hope of any material reward, but they sought the *summum bonum*, or the supreme good, for its own sake. For them, the *summum bonum* was the attainment of their union with God, Śiva. The aim of these mystics lay in the realization of and final absorption in God. They were called "Śaranas" simply because they sought their entire shelter in God.

These mystics did not merely preach morals, but acted accordingly. They found a parallel in Socrates in that they held knowledge and action as synonymous. They believed that a person who did a wrong was one who did not know the ethical code of conduct. In this belief they were enamoured more with faith and devotion than logic and rhetoric. For they said, "An action that is not based on knowledge is useless. It is like an action of the blind; what is the use of knowledge that does not result in good action? It amounts to the state of a lame person. To secure final absorption in God, knowledge and action both are necessary." Thus we find them effecting a harmonious blending of knowledge (*jnāna*) and action (*karma*). They assigned great value to moral motives transformed into good character. Basava, a leading philosopher-saint of Vīraśaivism, states, "I respect a person in saintly garb, but if he has no character befitting a saint, I discard him." For moral life, the quality of equanimity is essential. St. Prabhu (Allama Prabhu), whom Basava held in high esteem as his spiritual teacher, points out, "He is a real saint in whom the sense of high and low has disappeared." When a person is thus enlightened, the feeling of egotism is nipped in the bud. St. Cennabasava explains, "Egotism asserts material existence, but non-egotism asserts spiritual existence. Those who are shorn of egotism become one with God." To lead a moral life, it is necessary to keep the sensual desires under strict control.

1.   *Desire:* To ascend the first rung of the ladder of morality, one should give up desires for worldly pleasures. Desires increase our wants, and we tend to be greedy for material wealth and ignore our spiritual needs. If wants are not satisfied, it leads to frustraton, disappointment, and unhappiness. According to St. Urilingadeva, "Desires lead to slavery, want of desires lead to God-hood." Sister Mahādevi, in her quest of the Supreme Reality, expresses thus, "Just as a spider weaves a net out of the materials of its own body and is caught in the net and dies, so also do I worry myself by creating so many desires. O! God, clear away my mind from these filthy desires and show me the path leading towards you." St. Prabhu says, "Allay all passion, stop all sluggishness, blow up the mountain of your pride. If still your life is weltering in the world, how can you hope God will think your will is pure?" Even Basava laments:

> I am bound by the snare of desire, O Lord,
> I have no leisure to meditate on Thee.
> Bless me with Thy grace, Thou art kind,
> Beneficent and helpful in distress.[24]

Basava questions, "What if you perform the rigourous penance? Will the Lord have trust in those who are not pure of heart?" He also asked, "When once I know that the body, heart and wealth belong to God, is there for me another thought?"

Basava observed that greed and the desire for wealth are obstacles in the way of attaining the ultimate spiritual bliss. He professed that one should never be damned by greed. Like the moonlit glimmer of the night, wealth is fleeting and transient. But there is a supertransient state of mind if you dedicate yourself to God.

2.   *Anger:* Anger is an obstacle to moral progress. If a person falls prey to his or her senses and their objects, she/he becomes enamoured with them. From such attachment desires arise. If desires are not appeased, anger will follow. On account of anger, one loses balance of mind. From the loss of equanimity, one finds his/her reason missing. From the loss of reason she/he meets the destruction of self. Thus anger leads to so many evils in its chain of evils. Basava says, "Anger born of body spoils his own reputation. Anger born of mind spoils his own reason. O God! does not the fire of his own hearth burn his own house and not that of others?" The quality of forbearance adds luster to our good character. Sister Mahādevi emphasizes the need for sublimation of the senses, "This body is the abode of lust and lure, the shelter of arrogance and anger, thatched over with avarice and enmity. Unless these passions be sublimated, one knows not the Supreme Reality." Sister Mahādevi elaborates further, "Though the sandalwood is cut and rubbed, it does not cease to give fragrance with a grudge of being grated. Does the gold, even though cut into bits and melted in fire, cease to show its brightness? Does the sugarcane, even though cut into bits, crushed, squeezed, and turned into sugar, cease to give its sweetness? Is it a matter for personal loss if others pour, before my eyes, the fruits of my past life? O God! my father, were you to kill me, I will not abstain from worshipping you." These words of sister Mahādevi show how her heart was filled with extreme devotion and high moral character. Basava also expresses thus, "I shed lust, anger, greed, infatuation, envy, and pride — You are the cause!"

3.   *Self-control:* Senses are the root cause of all evil temptations. If the mind follows the fleeting senses, the mind is carried away just like the boat that is driven away by the storm. The better course would be to turn the mind toward God *(Linga),* and offer the material objects to God and then enjoy them as God's gifts. In this way bodily qualities in us vanish, and Godliness manifests itself. St. Ādayya has graphically described the states of the entangled and disentangled mind in this way, "He is happy who disentangles his mind from the snares of his senses. He is miserable who is swayed by his senses. He who turns his mind outward, is caught in the worldly illusion *(Māyā).* He who turns his mind inward, is considered an enlightened person. This is the way of making the senses sublime. One who reposes his mind solely in God, becomes liberated. If one's mind is entirely absorbed in God, he becomes one with God." These saints have professed and practiced gender equality. St. Devara Dāsimayya comments, "One who regards another's wife as goddess, will be born a king; and one who commits adultery with another's wife, will be thrown into hell." Furthermore, he maintains that the self is neither man nor woman. Basava appeals to God:

> Melt my mind, O Lord,
> And purge its stains.
> Test it and refine it in fire
> To pure gold this heart of mine![25]

4.   *Truth:* Adherence to the truth ennobles a person's character, and he or she will be held in high esteem by the public. A truthful man may suffer in this world, but truthful conduct is the basis for attaining spiritual goals. To speak falsehood is to cheat one's own self. The Vīraśaiva poet, Rāghavānka, believes that, "God is truth and truth is God." Basava also emphasizes, "To speak the truth is itself being in heaven on earth, and to speak falsehood is itself being in hell." Furthermore, Basava elaborates the importance of truth, purity of mind and conduct in the quest for the ultimate Reality.

> Heaven and earth are not different.
> Where there is truth there is heaven.
> Where there is deception there is mortal world.
> Pious conduct constitutes a paradise.
> Immoral behaviour is a hell in itself.[26]

> You swagggger upon an elephant,
> You groom yourself upon a horse,
> Your parade in saffron and in musk:
> And yet, alas! O brother,
> You are unaware of the Truth,
> You forgot to sow the seed and.
> nurture the plant of Virtue!
> Mounted upon the intoxicated elephant
> Of your immense pride,
> You are riding directly
> Into the snare of Destiny!
> Not knowing our Lord
> You only qualify for hell![27]

5.   *Honesty:* To refrain from stealing other's property is a great virtue, but Vīraśaiva saints were not content with this ethical principle. They believed that to earn more than what they required for their subsistence was an act not different from theft. St. Molige Mārayya maintained his livelihood by picking up rice grains scattered in the street. One day, when he had brought more rice than was required, his wife rebuked him and compelled him to return the excess rice. To keep the excess rice was as good as depriving others of food. These saints strictly adhered to the principles of dedicated work (*Kāyaka*), self-help and self-reliance, and community service (*Dāsoha*). To rely on others for their livelihood was considered by them as unethical and a serious breach of the Vīraśaiva work ethic. Basava says, "O, God! I pledge that I will touch neither a gold ornament nor a piece of cloth, for that is your command for me. If I fail to do so and desire others' property, O, God! throw me into the everlasting hell and discard me." Basava emphasized the need for purity and self-righteousness in our thoughts and actions.

> God is not pleased with those
> who have wicked motives but
> display humility in speech, and those
> whose deeds are not in conformity
> with their words.[28]

Your speech should be as pretty as a necklace
of pearls, as bright as a ruby; as spotless as a
crystal's flash, that cleaves the blue, and as truthful as
to be appreciated by God. But if your actions
should betray your words how can our Lord be
pleased?[29]

6.   *Nonviolence or Harmlessness:* Not to cause pain to others, either by evil motive or by words or actions is considered nonviolence or harmlessness (*Ahimsa*). St. Śanmukha swāmi states that, "When wise men speak, we should respond with humility. God departs from the place wherein harsh words are exchanged, just as fire arises when two stones collide with great force." This saying (*vacana*) lays emphasis on humility as a precious virtue. Purity of words and actions presuppose a pure mind. Basava questions, "How can God trust a man whose inner self is not pure?" Basava condemned animal sacrifice in strong terms, and has expressed pity for the animal thus, "O, goat! weep for your fate." He again comments, "A fisherman takes enjoyment in catching fish and killing them. Why does he not take pity on them as he does for the death of his own child? Is not that man worse than a butcher, who being a devotee of Śiva and yet slaughters living beings?" Basava has laid down a precept that compassion towards all living beings is the foundation of religion.

What sort of religion can it be
without compassion?
Compassion needs must be
Toward all living things;
Compassion is the root
of all religious faiths.[30]

7.   *Generosity:* To help others in their difficulty or distress is charity. Christianity asks us to regard our neighbors as ourselves. Vīraśaivism maintains that we regard our fellow neighbors as ourselves because the souls of all are one and the same. Even the birds and beasts assemble at a distress call of any one of their group. Basava exemplifies this social virtue in his saying, "Does not the crow, on seeing a crumb, call to its flock? Does not a hen, on seeing a morsel, make a call for its brood? A devotee of Śiva who lacks loyalty to his own faith is worse than a crow or hen." Charity or philanthropy advances the interest of the person who is charitable and of the person who is a beneficiary. Selfishness results in the aggrandizement of others and harms the reputation of the selfish person. The reward for charity is the love and blessing of the recipient. The selfish person's reward is the hatred incurred from others. What appears as compassion or humility in the field of morals, appears as devotion in the field of religion. One who is imbibed with devotion is unmindful of his body, mind, wealth, and life, and aspires for union with God. Basava, in his ecstatic state of devotion, has given vent to these admirable qualities of altruism or selflessness.

Make of my body, Lord
The beam for a lute;
Make of my head, the gourd;

> Make of my nerves the wires, O Lord,
> And of my fingers the plectrum make;
> Intone thy musical notes;
> O Lord, press my heart and play.[31]

These thoughts express the climax of self-sacrifice. Vīraśaiva saints combined in themselves both the qualities of preaching and of practising these principles. Basava has summarized all of these principles in his saying,

> Thou shalt not steal nor kill;
> Nor speak a lie;
> Be angry with no one,
> Nor scorn another person;
> Nor glory in yourself,
> Nor others hold to blame...
> This indeed is the way
> Of maintaining purity of mind
> And conduct,
> This is the way to win our Lord.[32]

Moreover, Basava stressed that one should lead an honest, pure, and righteous life to attain the ultimate union with God. One must work hard and earn one's living because there is no heaven apart from the pleasure of being absorbed in one's honest dedicated labor as a community service. These ethical principles form the main pillars of the Vīraśaiva religion and help to strengthen the bonds of the community's hold on individuals. The Vīraśaiva religious ethic provides a series of ideal patterns of behavior that do not always conform with its actual behavior patterns. Vīraśaiva psychology, theology, and philosophy, which are discussed in the subsequent chapters, show how ethical prinicples permeate every aspect of the devotee's life.

5

PSYCHOLOGICAL DIMENSIONS

The religious ideal of human beings is to think, speak, and act righteously, and thus qualify for the attainment of God. A religion that is based upon superstition fails to attract the rational mind. Science and religion seem to agree with regard to the Prime Substance out of which the universe is created. Issac Newton (Christianson, 1984; Manuel, 1974:48) equates space to the body of God: "The Supreme God is a Being eternal, infinite, absolutely perfect. He endures forever and is everywhere present; and by existing always and everywhere, he constitutes duration and space." Newton also argues that, "this most beautiful system of sun, planets, and comets could only proceed from the counsel and dominion of an intelligent and powerful Being." Thus Newton's universe was one of conscious design. Newton's scrutiny of nature was directed almost exclusively to the knowledge of God and not to the increase of sensate pleasure or comfort. Albert Einstein (1973) preferred to behave in an exactly engineered universe and frequently declared that "God does not play dice with the world." Furthermore, he (Bucky, 1992: 86) stated: "My religion consists of a humble admiration of the illimitable, superior spirit who reveals himself in the slight details we are able to perceive with our frail and feeble minds. That deeply emotional conviction of the presence of a superior reasoning power, which is revealed in the incomprehensible universe, forms my idea of God."

Religion professes to know and realize God by the faculty of intuition, while the reason of science confesses its inability to peep into the sphere of God and take an X-ray photograph of God. The cause for this seems to be that reason is born of matter, while intuition is born of the spirit. Vīraśaivism has contributed its own share to psychology. Its system of philosophy is called energy-qualified-monism (*Śaktivisistādwaita*). Before entering into the details of Vīraśaiva psychology, it is rather useful to briefly survey the principles of modern psychology in order to find the similarities in both of the systems. According to modern psychology, our nervous system is an electrochemical communication system that enables us to think, feel, and act. This nervous system is constructed of building blocks called neurons or nerve cells. The body's circuitry, the nervous system, consists of billions of cells, called neurons. The central nervous system's neurons in the brain and in the spinal cord communicate with the peripheral nervous system's sensory and motor neurons. This nervous system directs voluntary movements and reflexes, and controls our involuntary muscles and glands. By surgically lesioning electrically stimulating specific brain areas, by recording the brain's surface electrical activity, and by displaying neural activity with computer-aided brain scans, neuroscientists have explored the connections between brain, mind, and behavior.

Each of the brain's three basic regions — the brain stem, the limbic system, and the cerebral cortex — represents a stage of brain evolution. The brain stem begins where the spinal cord swells to form the medulla, which controls the heartbeat and breathing. The cerebellum, attached to the brain stem, coordinates muscle movement; within the brain stem, the reticular formation controls arousal and attention. On top of the brainstem is the thalamus, the brain's sensory switchboard. Between the brainstem and the cerebral cortex is the lymbic system, which has been linked primarily to memory, emotions, and drives. Also in the limbic system, the hypothalamus has been linked to various bodily maintenance functions, to pleasurable rewards, and to the control of the endocrine system, which affects emotional states, growth, and other body functions. Some brain regions are known to serve specific functions. In general, however, human emotions, thoughts, and behavior result from the intricate coordination of many brain areas.

Just as modern psychology has made three divisions of the brain, so also has Vīraśaivism created three parts in the brain. It calls the frontal brain by the name of *Brahmarandra*. It consists of a thousand petals or groups of nerves. In this part the intellectual consciousness aspect of God (*Citkala*) dwells in the form of self (*Jiva*). This self (*Jiva*) is a formless God called *Niśkalalinga*. The central part of the brain is called *Sikhácakra*. This consists of three groups of nerves. In this part life-breath (*Prāna*) dwells and is named God of the Void (*Sūnyalinga*). The hind part of the brain is called *Pascimacakra*, which consists of a single nerve. In this part, the self-luminous soul dwells and is called God Without Attributes (*Niranjanalinga*). Just below this part, the spinal cord joins. Thus we find a curious coincidence between the Vīraśaiva and modern psychological descriptions of the brain.

Vīraśaiva psychology has proceeded a step further, and has divided the nervous system of the human body into six parts: (1) middle of the eyebrows, (2) neck, (3) heart, (4) navel, (5) the generating organ, and (6) the excreting organ. These are the places where the important nerves are located, and each of them performs a particular function. The nerve ending in the middle of the eyebrows is called *Ājnacakra*. This operates as an efferent nerve in communicating the commands of the brain to the different sense organs. The neck contains the nerve (*Vishuddhicakra*), wherein lies ether, which enables the esophagus (food carrying valve) to send the food down to the stomach, enables the larynx (soundvalve) to create sound, and enables the trachea lying below the larynx to breathe.

In the heart, the *Anāhatacakra* is situated, wherein lies the airy principle that helps to purify blood flowing into the heart from various parts of the body and then discharge it to various parts. The navel contains *Manipurakacakra*, wherein lies the fiery principle that subjects the bowels to contraction and expansion, helping to bring about the digestion of food. The generating organ contains *Swādisthānacakra*, wherein lies the principle of the earth. The heart, trachea, and brain are important organs, and if they are severely damaged, life passes away. There are five sense organs *(jnānendriyas)*: (1) the eye, (2) the nose, (3) the tongue, (4) the ear, and (5) the skin. The functions of these organs should be sublimated.

The eye can see both the ugly and the beautiful. An aspirant *(bhakta)* of God *(Linga* or *Śiva)* endeavors to refrain from an evil look. To accomplish this objective, he starts with the hypothesis that God exists in each sense organ, and whatever is worthy and conducive to moral and spiritual progress should be seen, smelt, tasted, heard, and touched. The idea of the existence of God *(Linga)* in each sense organ prevents the aspirant from becoming a slave to the senses, and saves him from doing what is wrong. Thus the devotee is fully imbibed with the idea of Godhood and habituates himself to act like God. He becomes a God-like person. Whatever he does, he does it without expecting rewards.

The *Isha Upanishad* says that the whole world is permeated with God *(Śiva* or *Linga)*, and whatever is given by Him, we should accept, and that we should not covet the wealth of others. This principle forms the nucleus upon which the Vīraśaiva psychology has developed its own system. Thus Vīraśaivism posits the existence of *Śivalinga* in the eye, *Ācāralinga* in the nose, *Gurulinga* in the tongue, *Prasādalinga* in the ear, and *Caralinga* in the skin. So it sublimates every sense organ by investing it with a *Linga*. Having a pure and sincere mind is the only means of reaching the moral and spiritual heights. Vīraśaiva beliefs are based on psychological and spiritual premises. St. Cennabasava says, "People say that body should not be divested of God *(Linga)*. What is the use of body and the symbol of God (*Linga)* being together if the mind is not concentrated on God *(Śiva)*?" This saying indicates that the outward act of wearing *Linga* on the body is useless if the mind is not absorbed in God *(Śiva)*.

Vīraśaiva psychology regards mind and reason as the offsprings of the brain and hence born of matter, and they derive their power and inspiration from the soul *(Jiva)*. Even life-breath *(Prāna)* is a material object, although it is subtle and invisible to the naked eye. It is one of the five elements. It sustains the body as long as it receives inspiration from the soul *(Jiva)*, and it stops functioning as soon as the soul *(Jiva)* leaves the body. Vīraśaivism holds that the soul *(Jiva)* is not a material thing, but a spiritual entity. It is a spark of God Almighty. It will find its oneness with God when it undergoes a spiritual journey.

According to Vīraśaivism, the prototype symbol of God on the body (the *istalinga)* is a mere witness of the actions of the soul *(Jiva)*, which finds its liberation from the world's entanglements and realizes its identity with God. This is the state of the God realized person *(the Aikya)* attaining oneness with God *(Śiva)*. In the Dualism *(Dwaita)*, as avowed by Mádhawa (Embree, 1966), the individual self *(Jivātma)* is not God *(Paramātma)*; one is the servant and the other is the master. In the Monism *(Advaita)*, as represented by Śankara, although the identities of the individual self *(Jivātma)* and God *(Paramātma)* are maintained, the monism exposes itself to a fallacy by saying that the world is unreal (*Māyā*). If this were so, how can it account for the existence of the real individual self (*Jivātma*) in an unreal body? The qualified monism (*visisthādwaita*), founded by Rāmānuja, states that the individual self (*Jivātma*) can achieve qualities akin to God, but does not secure oneness with God. This view ascribes imperfection to the souls (*Jivas*). The energy-qualified-monism (the *Śaktivisisthādwaita)*, as propounded by Vīraśaivism, maintains that the individual self (*Jivātma*) is essentially one with God (*Paramātma*), and that the world is real as it is created and permeated by God. These four schools admit the immortality of the soul, but differ as to its final relationship with God.

Vīraśaiva psychology finds a parallel in modern psychology in maintaining the theory of interactionism. According to this theory, body and mind act on one another. When I wish to light a candle I strike a matchstick. This action takes place not by mere movements of the nerves, but essentially by my wish. Under the command of the will, the nerves of the brain will move and cause the fingers to contract and then strike the matchstick. Similarly, the body acts on the mind. When the body is sick, the mind suffers and becomes uneasy. For this reason, Vīraśaivism enjoins the duty of carrying out good deeds and maintaining purity of action by the body and purity of thought of the mind untill the end of life. It prohibits its votaries from speaking falsehoods, thinking ill of others, and committing fornication, theft, and murder.

The six spiritual stages (*Śatsthalas*) of Vīraśaivism also are based on psychological and spiritual principles. (1) The Devotion stage (*Bhaktasthala*) lays down a condition on the devotee (men or women) of sacrificing their body, mind, and wealth for their spiritual guide (*Guru*), God (*Linga*), and the itenerant religious mentor (*Jangama*). (2) In the Master of discipline (*Maheshsthala*) stage, the devotee does all actions without a desire for their fruits, and regards all living beings like his own self. (3) In the receiver of Grace (*Prasādisthala)* stage, the devotee first offers all things to God and then enjoys them as God's gifts. He ascribes all of his actions to God, being prompted by God, and, in fact, identifies himself with God. (4) In the Linga, in the life-breath (*Prānalingsthala)*i stage, the devotee regards life (*Prāna)* as God's energy, and considers the concentration of his mind on *Prānalinga* to be his ideal. In this stage, union with Śiva *(Śivayoga)* is attained. (5) In the life divine (*Śaranasthala*) stage, the devotee regards oneself as the wife and God as the husband, and takes entire shelter in God. The devotee lives and moves and has his/her being in God. (6) In the union with the Godhead (*Aikya*) stage, the devotee loses the feeling of individual existence by having fully merged in God's personality. This final stage is expressed by the simile of camphor being consumed by the fire. The camphor leaves no residue, not even an atom of ashes when burnt by the fire. Many Vīraśaiva saints describe this ultimate union with God as the process of milk merging with milk, light merging with light, space merging with space, and so forth. Basava describes this indescribable stage thus:

> Look at the Being
> that persists when all
> the mirky darkness is dispelled!
> When light has been
> enthroned on light,

Lord Śiva alone knows
the Union of light
when wedded into Light.
O Lord
the inner and the outer
are now one
soul united into Soul.[33]

So these six stages represent the gradual development of the mind until the sixth rung of the ladder leads one to the climax of the spiritual heights. The Vīraśaiva devotees regard their whole body as being pervaded by God *(Linga)*, and all of their actions as being directed by God. No evil deed can proceed from the devotee, and hence the belief that there is no rebirth for one who has reached the final stage of the spiritual journey.

St. Molige Mārayya states: "Purity of action is a first step to secure purity of mind. If mind is pure, soul *(Ātma)* is pure. If soul *(Ātma)* is pure, one's consciousness is fully saturated with Godliness." St. Śivalenka Mancanna professes, "One should worship the God *(Linga)* until his life *(Prāna)* is imbibed with Godliness." These teachings lay emphasis on the mental contemplation of God. Vīraśaivism discards idol worship. Worship of Śiva in temples is prohibited. It does not recognize the ascetic discipline *(yogic exercises)* of Patanjali. Righteous behavior is as good as practising spiritual exercise *(yoga)*. The aim of Vīraśaivism is to sublimate the senses and other astral and causal faculties in humans by investing them with God (*Linga)*, thus enabling them to dazzle with divine sparks. The spiritual preceptor *(Guru)* makes the devotee aware of the existence of the intelligent aspect of God *(Citkala)* lying latent in his hindbrain, and gives it to him in the form of an emblem of God Śiva *(Istalinga)* for his worship. This prototype of God Śiva *(Linga)* is a means to attain God who is without name and form. God pervades the whole world, even the gross matter that, being the creation of God, is subject to divine laws. Matter is one of the thirty-six principles or categories (Malledevaru, 1973) in the Vīraśaiva cosmological system. It is one of the ingredients out of which the whole universe is created. It is different from soul *(Ātma)*.

Sānkhya philosophy regards matter to be as eternal as the soul, but Vīraśaivism as energy-qualified-monism *(śaktivisistādwaita)* makes the eternity of matter dependent on God and subjects it to God's evolutionary process. According to the Sānkhya philosophy, matter *(Prakrti)* acts so long as it is in the presence of the soul *(Puruśa)*, even though the soul *(Puruśa)* is inactive and does not inspire matter. If this is so, how can the Sānkhya philosophy ascribe activity to a substance that has no initiative or self-activity? Vīraśaivism provides a content, namely the symbol of Śiva *(Linga)*, through the contemplation of which the formless God is realized. Souls are eternal and they emanate from God, just as the rays of the sun spread out at sunrise. Souls are full of divine energy *(the Śakti)*. Matter is a creation of God, just as the web of the spider is a creation of the spider out of its body. The foregoing analysis demonstrates that the Vīraśaiva thinkers have taken a rationalistic point of view in linking body, mind, and soul to the divine.

6

THEOLOGY OF VĪRAŚAIVISM

Theology deals with the existence, nature, and attributes of God. Theology begins with a faith in the divine, and tries to work out the implications of this for human life and the ways in which human experience helps us to understand the nature of divine being within a particular religious tradition (Scharf, 1971:11). Since the dawn of society the idea of God has taken root in the minds of human beings. A great number of people believed firmly that there must be a first cause or creator for this wonderful creation. However, through all the ages there have been some people who have had no belief in the existence of God. The Cārvākas among the Hindus, Epicurus and Democritus among the Greeks, Sir Charles Bradlaw among the British, and Ingersoll among the Americans, are known to be atheists of the first magnitude. These thinkers say that the manifold creation is due to the various combination of different atoms. If we do not admit the existence of a first cause, we will be arguing in a circle, just as we do in tracing the cause of the tree in the seed and of the seed in the tree. So there will be no end to our thinking.

A modern evolutionist, when tracing the origin of a chicken, argues that it has evolved through many stages by attributing its origin to a living organism that itself arose from nature. The Vīraśaiva thinkers, however, recognize that the energy working in nature is nothing but the intelligent power or energy of God (Śiva-śakti). The highest intelligent human being, as well as an atom of dust, the microcosm (Pindānda), as well as the macrocosm (Brahmānda), are permeated by divine energy. Owing to this very idea, the Vīraśaiva philosophy is known as energy-qualified-monism. (Śaktivisistādwaita).

Just as we necessarily presume the existence of a sculptor for a beautifully carved statue, so also do we have to presume the existence of an omniscient, omnipotent, and omnipresent being for the creation and guidance of the universe that is regulated by uniform laws. This is a statement from the point of view of cause and effect. From the moral standpoint, we tend to think that our good or bad deeds will lead to good or bad consequences. But to shape the future life and apportion adequate fruits to every soul for its actions (*karma*), a divine judge is inevitable. Earth, water, fire, air, and sky, by their own cooperation, cannot create an earthen pot. A potter is necessary for its creation. An evolutionist, with the help of any number of elements, is unable to create life endowed with its particular body. There are many things beyond the comprehension of human intellect. Human beings have not yet been able to perfectly comprehend the nature of their own minds and souls. We can only infer that our mind exists from the power of its thinking, and our soul from the action of breathing and from the revival of the former memory and consciousness after we awaken from an absolutely sound sleep. Mind and soul are not things to be seen by the eye. When the soul departs from the body, all bodily activities will be put to an end, and the body will become as motionless as a log of wood. So we establish and determine the nature and existence of invisible energies such as electricity, radio waves, or the microwave by the actions resulting from them. We have to adopt the same method with regard to the existence of God.

The Vīraśaiva philosophical system maintains that the universe is created by the energy of God. Some scientists, such as Issac Newton, Albert Einstein, J. S. Haldane, and several others have held the same view. For instance, Newton considered Principia and Optics, his two major books, to be useful since they had helped to make manifest the laws of God, and had revealed His nature. They think that there is divine energy or consciousness in every atom, that thought is not a mere overt action of the brain, but a result of the inner energy, and that this energy can persist and survive even after the cessation of the brain's activity or the death of human beings. They have further expressed that there is an Almighty God who can unify all the diversities existing in the universe. The study of plant life made by biologists demonstrates the same truth. According to James Jeans, the gross things cannot remain constant, and there is a constant spiritual factor that is the pivot of the whole universe. So the materialistic view of the evolutionists, such as Charles Darwin, Professor Haeckel, and others, has been questioned.

Among the six philosophical systems (*Śatdarshanas*) of India, the Mimāmsa, Vedānta, Yoga, Nyāya, and Vaiśesika systems (Radhakrishnan and Moore, 1967) believe in the existence of God. The Sānkhya system does not propose the existence of God. In Sānkhya there is a conception of innumerable souls (*purusas*). This view finds a parallel in Jainism, which asserts the existence of a plurality of perfected souls instead of a single supreme Being. According to Buddha (an agnostic), we are unable to know whether or not God exists. Kanāda, the author of the Vaiśesika School of philosophy, maintains the idea that the universe is created from a combination of various kinds of atoms, and holds that God impells every atom to function. Bādarāyana, the author of Vedānta, affirms that God is the creator of the nature of goodness, intelligence, and bliss. He pleaded monism (*adwaita*) by saying that God and soul are one. In the dualism (*dwaita*) of the Madhwa School, God is the master and the soul is the servant, and this difference is to last forever. In the qualified monism (*Visistādwaita*) of the Rāmānuja School, the soul does not fully realize its oneness in God, but assumes a form similar to that of God. In the Vīraśaiva School of philosophy, the soul, after reaching the ultimate spiritual stage, attains absolute oneness with God (*Lingānga Sāmarasya*).

God is named as Sthala, Śiva, and Linga. The one God differentiates himself as an emblem (*Istalinga*) on the devotee's body, as "Prānalinga" in the heart, and as "Bhāvalinga" in the mind. When one looks into the mirror he sees himself and his reflection. When the mirror is removed, both forms are merged therein. Likewise, a person who has achieved the synthesis of knowledge and action, being dissolved in God (*Linga*), becomes God (*Linga*) alone. God is with form and without form. St. Siddharāma illustrates, "O God, thou art like a tree and its seed, the tree being invisible in the seed." Basava remarks, "Thou art a self-created Being, possessing mysterious powers and one beyond the reach of mind or speech, a Being smaller than the smallest and greater than the greatest." God permeates the whole universe and yet He is untainted by terrestrial impurities.

To Spinoza (a pantheist), God and the world are synonymous. The world is God and God is the world. Vīraśaivism has escaped from this fallacy by holding that, although God is immanent, He is transcendent. So Vīraśaivism has maintained a suprapantheistic view. God manifests himself in a person who has acquired perfect knowledge. Such a person is fit to be worshipped. St. Devara Dāsimayya says, "O, God! This earth and its harvest are thy gifts. The wind that blows around us is thy gift. What can I say of those who enjoy thy gifts but are not devoted to thee?"

God has many attributes. He is without cause (*upādhi*). He is brilliant light (*Paranjyoti*), one beyond comparison, eternal and all perfect. According to St. Urilingadeva, God is the inspirer of all things, and without his initiation, not even a blade of grass moves. God possesses mysterious powers. St. Devara Dāsimayya describes "O God! you balanced the earth on the waters and kept it from melting away, you made the sky stand without pillar or foundation; you concealed fire in the wood so as not to be kindled of its own accord, ghee in the milk so that its taste may not be felt, and kept the soul in the body so as not to be visible. I am astounded at the mixture of opposites created by Thee!" God is not affected by the sins of human beings, just as the sun's reflection in the water is not affected by the water, and just as the lotus flower, though stemming in a pond, remains above water.

With a desire to create the world, God differentiated himself into many souls. This is the creative path of engagement (*pravrtti Mārga*) of his energy. The soul, being entangled in the world, aspires to attain God through the path of devotion. This is the path of deliverance or disengagement (*nivrtti Mārga*). Energy (*Śakti*) and devotion (*Bhakti*) ultimately become one and their difference vanishes. In this way, Vīraśaivism brings about a harmony between dualism (*Dwaita*) and monism (*Adwaita*). Its fundamental doctrine is that energy (*Śakti*) is God (*Linga*), devotion (*Bhakti*) is soul (*Anga*), and the union of both is the *summum bonum*. St. Ambigara Chaudayya points out that God certainly dwells in the heart of one who is pure in thought, word, and deed. Mahadeviyamma, the wife of St. Molige Mārayya, addresses: "O God! thou art infallibly present where truth and faith are present." God is one without a second. St. Sanmukha swāmi compares that God is one just as there is one sun, but appears as many when reflected in many ponds. God is formless. Idols are not to be worshipped. But the symbol of God (*Istalinga*), worn on the body, is to be worshipped as a manifestation of God's energy (*Śakti*). According to Basava, idols are not God; but if one were to realize his Self, he becomes aware of his own divinity. For constant remembrance of God, one must wear the symbol of God (*Linga*) on his body. St. Prabhu says, "One should realize the Supreme Being although remaining in a physical frame made up of five elements. To realize that Being, a symbol is necessary. If one wishes to realize God, the Supreme Being is in one's own heart" St. Cennabasava asserts that the symbol of God (*Istalinga*), is like a mirror, and the devotee sees the reflection of God in it. This symbol (*Istalinga*) is only a means for realizing God, for St. Prabhu indicates that if one loses this symbol of God (*Istalinga*) Linga in the heart (*Pranalinga*) is not lost. Basava has stressed the importance of prayer and worship of the symbol of God (*Istalinga*): "O God! I am like a bee tasting the fragrance of Thy lotus-like feet; while my speech is filled with the nectar of thy name and my eyes filled with thy splendid form, my mind is saturated with thy remembrance and my ears are filled with the sound of Thy glory."

In the Vīraśaiva system there is no separate existence of a heaven apart from the world. St. Siddharāma says that, "If one realizes Linga after experiencing the hollowness of the senses and their qualities, he finds himself as if placed in heaven (*Kailāsa*) and becomes one with God." Such a devotee is not reborn. A devotee's body is a temple of God. Kant, the German idealist, maintains that God (Thing in itself) is the only real thing, but that his nature is beyond comprehension. Śankara, the Hindu idealist, likewise argues that God alone is real and the world is illusion or unreal (*Māyā*). Such absolute idealism of both philosophers is opposed to science and reason. Vīraśaivism affirms the reality of the world as it is created by God. God permeates every atom in the world and is the propeller in everything. Berkeley, an absolute idealist, asserts that the only things that exist and are real are those that are seen by the senses (*esse est percipi*), and those that are not so perceived have no existence.

Vīraśaivism states that the soul, although not perceived by the senses, is apprehended by the eye of knowledge and its existence inferred by its actions, and that none can relate its nature after it is merged in God. Soul is a real entity in the body, and through its inspiration and illumination the eyes see, the tongue speaks, the ears hear, the nose smells and so on. The world is created by God through his energy and is guided by the law of energy, which the scientists call "the law of nature." Basava professes that "God is one but his names are many." Everything is the creation of God and everything finally finds its absorption in God.

7

VĪRAŚAIVA PHILOSOPHY

The Vīraśaiva philosophy, metaphysics, and cosmology appear to be complex, especially the highly differentiated categories about the different kinds of lingas, angas, śaktis, and bhaktis, and about the various substages of the principle six-phase spiritual system. Metaphysics, as a branch of philosophy, investigates the principles of the reality that underlies the phenomena in the universe. There lies beneath the changing phenomena a real substratum that is constant and everlasting, and which is the cause of creation and destruction. This reality is self-created, and employs its energy in shaping and moulding the universe in all its aspects of movable and immovable objects. Vīraśaivism believes that the world is real, being the creation of God. Just as the spider creates its web out of the materials of its own body, God creates the world by His will for His own play and dissolves it within Himself. God (*Linga*), by His will, changed Himself into the two aspects of energy (*Śakti* or *māyā*) and devotion (*bhakti*). By the Lord's engagement (*pravrtti*) through energy, the process of creation and evolution of the universe takes place. The energy (*śakti*) creates desire among all human beings, and they are subject to the limitations of time, space, causation, and pleasure and pain. Through devotion (*bhakti*), the process of involution or disengagement (*nivrtti*) occurs. The liberation of the soul (*anga*) is possible only when, through devotion, it seeks to attain God (*Linga*). Both energy (*śakti*) and devotion (*bhakti*) are powers of the Lord and represent evolution and involution, respectively.

The paths of energy and devotion may be aptly compared to the soul's downward and upward ways of Heracleitus, the Greek philosopher. Alhough God is the creator and permeates the world, He is free from all limitations, just as the lotus flower is not moistened by water even though it grows in it. God is immanent in all things and yet manifests Himself more in the moving substance than in the gross, still more clearly in intelligent life, and most clearly in human beings. Souls are related to one another as they emanate from one and the same God. All souls finally find their oneness in the same God. So everyone should regard others as members of the same family, and any harm done to one of them is as good as harming oneself. When the soul is free from desires it is united with God. Just as a camphor, when burnt, leaves no ashes, so the soul finds its complete absorption in God.

According to the Vīraśaiva cosmology, the Supreme Soul in the form of Śiva or Linga is the only real eternal entity. Even before time and creation, it is first a self-subsistent Void or Space (*śūnya, bayalu*). It is perfect, serene, sustained, inaccessible to knowledge, beyond illusion, immaculate, and absolute. This Supreme Reality exists with neither beginning, middle, nor end. In the evolution, the Absolute Void becomes the Śūnya Linga, self-generated and impartite. This pure and absolute Godhead exists before there is body and mind or life and death, thought and knowledge, before existence, consciousness, and bliss.

This Śūnya Linga, through its spontaneous "sport" (*lilā*), becomes the Great Linga (*Mahālinga*) that is the all-pervasive, undivided, mass of Light (*belagu*). The Great Linga is identical with the sacred word Ōm; this Supreme Effulgent Linga shines brilliantly with the light of infinite billions of suns.

The Great Linga was by itself alone and not conscious of Itself; became the Consciousness with the attributes of existence, consciousness, bliss, perfection, and eternity; and became the formless Śiva-principle. The Great Linga, for His own spontaneous sport and by mere vibration of its energy, divided into soul (*Anga*) and God (*Linga*). God (*Linga*) and energy, or power (*Śakti*), are inseparable, and soul (*Anga*) and devotion (*bhakti*) are linked together. Linga, Anga, and Śakti each assumed six modes (see Figure 7.1).

The formless Śiva-principle, in order to create the world, evolved into the Linga-Anga differentiation, from which five elements that constitute matter and the entire universe arose. When the soul assumed a body, we had the beginnings of creation and, later, consciousness, including the knowledge of the Divine. Linga is Siva and the soul (*Anga*) is the devotee (*Śarana*). The Vīraśaiva philosophers and mystics maintain that God (*Linga*) and soul (*Anga*) are essentially one and the same but manifest the difference in the initial stage of the spiritual journey of a devotee. But when the soul, realizing its nature, resorts to spiritual pursuits through devotion, the six-phase system, eight aids, and the fivefold socio-ethical codes of conduct, the distinction between God and soul gradually decreases. In the final stage of the spiritual journey, the individual soul (*Anga*) becomes one with the Universal Soul (*Linga*).

The fundamental Virasaiva philosophy stresses that the individual's goal is eventual unity with Śiva, the Supreme Reality. The individual soul (*anga*), through disengagement, dedicated selfless work (*kāyaka*), and devotion (*bhakti*) for the Linga, has to go through the six spiritual stages in order to attain unity with Śiva (*Linga*), the integral associaton of God and soul (*Lingānga sāmarasya*).

In the Vīraśaiva theism, the Supreme Reality (*Śiva*) is characterized by the epithets of (see Figure 7.1) existence (*sat*), consciousness or intelligence (*cit*), and bliss (*ānanda*), and He is called "Sthala." The universe exists in the Supreme Reality (*ParaŚiva or Brahman*). The universe emerged from matter (*prakrti*) and soul (*puruśa*), and it ultimately leads to dissolution. For this reason Lord Śiva is called "Sthala." The first part, "Stha," signifies situation, and the second part, "la," signifies

Figure 7.1
The Six-Phase Spiritual System

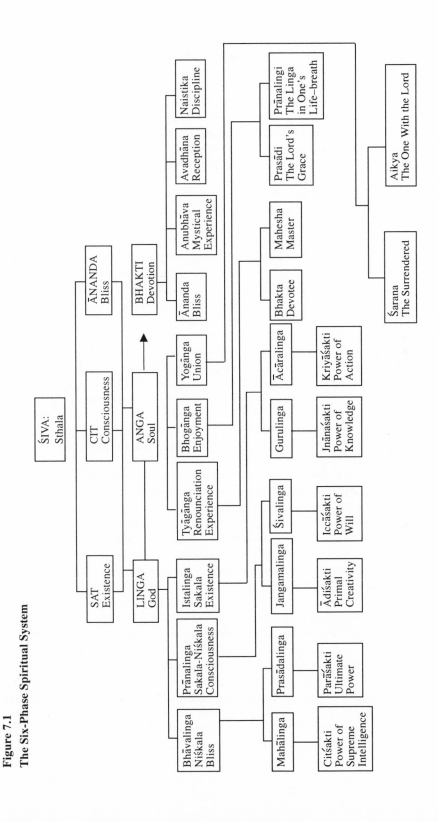

"Laya" or dissolution. It is called "Sthala" because He is the support of the whole movable and immovable universe, and He holds all powers, all luminaries, and all souls. The Vīraśaiva mystics also use terms such as Bayalu, Sūnya, or Linga to denote the Supreme Reality. He is higher than the highest, one without a second, and the resting place of all. The devotee seeks the ultimate happiness in uniting with Śiva.

By the agitation of its innate primeval energy (*Śakti*) Sthala divides itself into two aspects — (1) God (*Lingasthala*) and (2) individual soul (*Angasthala*). The energy of Śiva that is vested in the Linga is called "Śakti." The same energy vested in "Anga"(soul) is called "Bhakti" (devotion). "Śakti" leads to activity and finds itself entangled with the world. Bhakti is free from this susceptibility, and turning away from action leads one to ultimate liberation. The "Śakti" in the Linga is an object of worship. The "Śakti" in the "Anga," that is "Bhakti," makes one a worshipper.

Śiva, the Supreme Reality, who is beyond all attributes, assumed form because of His own desire or play (*lilā*) to help devotees. The Linga is Śiva Himself, and not a mere symbol of Him. The Linga appears in three forms — (1) bhāvalinga, (2) prānalinga, and (3) istalinga. The Bhāvalinga is without any parts, the Absolute (*niśkala*), and is to be perceived by faith. It is mere existence (*sat*), conditioned by neither space nor time. It is self-existent, formless, blissful, eternal, and perfect in all respects. The distinction between the worshipper and the worshipped is felt in the initial stage. This distinction between the individual soul (*anga*) and the Linga (*Śiva*) gradually disappears as the devotee undergoes, with the help of the eightfold shields and by adhering to the five codes of conduct, the six-phase spiritual system (*satsthalas*). The Prānalinga is to be apprehended by the mind, and is both with and without parts (*sakala-niśkala*). Istalinga is with parts (*sakala*) and is apprehended by the eye. It is called "ista" because it confers all desired objects and banishes afflictions. The Prānalinga is the intelligence, or consciousness, and bhāvalinga, the bliss of the supreme God.

Each of these three Lingas is again divided into two. Bhāvalinga is divided into mahālinga, and prasādalinga, and prānalinga divides itself into jangamalinga and Śivalinga. Istalinga divides itself into gurulinga and acaralinga. When the essence of Śiva is operated on by the power of intelligence (*cit-śakti*) it forms mahālinga, the attributes of which are the absence of birth, death, freedom from taint, and so forth. When the essence of Śiva gets permeated with its supreme power (*parā-śakti*), a principle called sādakhya, which is light, eternal, indivisible, imperceptible to the senses, and indestructible, emerges. This principle is called prasādalinga. When the essence of Śiva is operated on by its primeval power (*ādi-śakti*), cara or jangama linga is produced, which is infinite and pervades the internal and external worlds. It is full of light, it is soul (*puruśa*), and it is higher than matter (*prakrti*); it is capable of being contemplated by the mind alone. When permeated by will power (*iccā-śakti*), it forms Śivalinga, which is a finite principle with a sense of egoism. It is possessed of knowledge and power, and has a celestial effulgence. When permeated with the power of knowledge (*jnāna-śakti*), it forms gurulinga, which presides over every system or science that instructs. It is full of light, a boundless ocean of joy, and dwells in human intelligence. When influenced by the power of action (*kriyā-śakti*), it is called ācāralinga, which, in the shape of action, serves as the support for the existence of all things. It is conceivable by the mind, and leads to a life of renunciation.

These six forms are various aspects of God. By the first form, we consider Him as creator. By the second we regard Him as pure intelligence. By the third He is thought of as distinct from the material world. By the fourth He is conceived of as having a body, not of ordinary matter but of celestial. By the fifth He is regarded as instructing humanity. By the sixth He is considered to be a guide for the individual souls until they are liberated. Śiva is regarded as the redeemer.

Devotion (*bhakti*) is a tendency of love toward God. There are three stages in the progress of this tendency, and corresponding to these are three kinds of souls (*anga*): (1) yogānga, (2) bhogānga, and (3) tyāgānga. By yogānga, a devotee obtains happiness by his/her union with Śiva. By bhogānga, the devotee enjoys along with Śiva. Tyāgānga is the abandonment or renunciation of the world as transient. Yogānga includes two stages, śarana and aikya. Śarana is a devotee who has sought his/her entire shelter in God. The devotee sees God in his/herself and in everything else. Such devotion is called devotion of bliss (*ānanda bhakti*). An aikya is a devotee who has realized his/her oneness with God. Such devotion is called devotion of oneness (*samarasa bhakti*), in which God and soul are united. Bhogānga includes the prānalingi and prasādi stages. The prānalingi stage consists of abandoning all regard for life, renunciation of egoism, and concentration of the mind solely on Linga. Such devotion is called heartfelt devotion (*anubhāva bhakti*). The Prasādi stage is realized when one resigns all objects of his/her enjoyment to the Linga. Such devotion is called concentrated devotion (*avadhāna bhakti*). Tyāgānaga includes the mahesh and bhakta stages. A mahesh is one who has a firm faith in the existence of God, and who undergoes the strict discipline of observing the vows of truth, morality, cleanliness, compassion for living beings, and so forth. This kind of devotion is called firm faith devotion (*nishtā bhakti*). A devotee (*bhakta*) is one who, turning his/her mind away from all objects, practices devotion and lives a life of detachment from the mundane pleasures and pains. This type of devotion is called deep devotion (*naistika* or *śraddhā bhakti*). This spiritual process goes on progressing until it reaches the Aikya stage, where the soul finds its absolute oneness with God, representing the ultimate depersonalization of the individual soul beyond the cycle of birth and death. The soul returns to the Divine Void from which it had originally emerged. The devotee (*bhakta, Śárana or anga*) and Linga (*Śiva*) become one. There is nothing to medidate upon, no God, no devotee. One is transformed into the Divine. This state of Oneness is like water merging with water and like space merging with space.

These are the six stages (*śatshalas*) of spiritual progress. Several Vīraśaiva philosophers-saints have emphasized the perfect identity between the Supreme and the individual soul. St. Śanmukha swāmi describes this state of ultimate union: "O my Lord! Now I have no body to worship Thee, for You assume my body. I have no mind to meditate upon Thee as it is merged in Thine. I have no consciousness to apprehend Thee for that consciousness is absorbed by Thee like the camphor consumed by fire." Basava describes the joy and bliss of union with Śiva: "O Lord, the inner and the outer are now one, soul married into soul. How can I tell the way the word that 'I am' within the lofty light Śiva has been turned to Silence?" This clearly shows perfect identity beyond doubt. The final beatitude (*kaivalya*) of the Vīraśaivas represents the complete oneness of the soul with God, for that soul is never reborn.

In the following verse, St. Prabhu narrates about the highest stage of mystical experience:

> The motion of the will is still!
> All words are dedicated to Him.
> Nay, language has no trace of sound;
> Nor is there in all space abound —
> As soon as the word Śiva
> In the soul is heard.[34]

> Waiting for your Vision,
> I gazed:
> it was like the instantaneous dawn
> of a million million suns,
> a trillion of thunderbolts
> to my amazement.
> O Lord,
> if you are the effulgent light
> there is no metaphor.[35]

St. Cennabasava describes the harmony of devotion, knowledge, and action and the state of union of the individual soul with the Supreme Soul:

> The spaceless body is lost in unity;
> The spaceless mind is lost in unity;
> The spaceless will is lost in unity;
> The void, absorbing void, is now redirected
> To void; the very word
> Lord Śiva too has vanished![36]

Śiva is omniscient, but soul (*anga or jiva*) is of limited knowledge. The soul that is deluded by nescience or ignorance (*Avidyā*), forgets God and is caught in the snares of the world. Only when the soul pursues the path of devotion (*bhakti*), does God liberate the soul by His grace. The soul will have to discard three impurities born of atoms *(ānavamala)*, born of illusion (*māyāmala*), and born of action (*kārmikamala*) before it can be emancipated. The devotee will have to pass through three acts of purification or initiation (*dīkśa*). When the teacher lays his hand on the head of the devotee, believing it to be the seat of God, it is called *vedha dīkśa*. When the teacher utters prayers into the ears of the devotee, it is called *mantra dīkśa*. When the teacher places the symbol of Śiva (*Linga*) in the hands of the devotee, it is called *kriya dīkśa*.

The devotee will have to accept eight coverings, shields or aids (*astāvaranas*) (see Figure 7.2) for the purification of his or her body and mind. The devotee is expected to: (1) select a preceptor (*Guru*) for guidance in reaching spiritual goals; (2) always wear a symbol of God (*Linga*) on the body, given by the preceptor (*Guru*); (3) approach and worship an itinerant religious teacher (*Jangama*) and acquire spiritual wisdom from him; (4) accept the holy water poured over the Guru's feet (*pādodaka*);

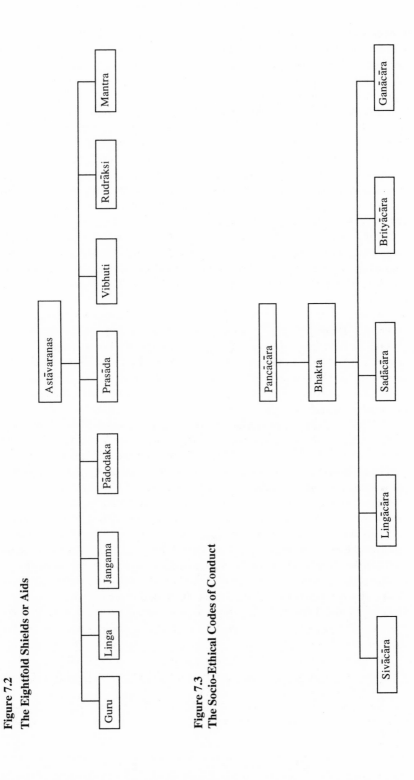

Figure 7.2
The Eightfold Shields or Aids

Aṣṭāvaraṇas

Guru Liṅga Jaṅgama Pādodaka Prasāda Vibhuti Rudrākṣi Mantra

Figure 7.3
The Socio-Ethical Codes of Conduct

Pañcācāra
Bhakta

Sivācāra Liṅgācāra Sadācāra Brityācāra Ganācāra

(5) accept gifts of food or grace (*prasāda*) from the Guru; (6) anoint one's body with holy ashes (*vibhuti*); (7) wear rosary (*rudrāksi*) on one's body; and (8) recite prayers (*mantras*) instructed by one's Guru. These sacred symbols and rituals tend to create an ethos, a set of feelings and motivations that make the religious worldview seem uniquely realistic for devotees.

The devotee should also observe the five socio-ethical codes of conduct (*pancācāras*) (see Figure 7.3). (1) The devotee should regard all members of the Śiva community as equal. Even if a person is an untouchable by birth, that person should be regarded as a devotee of Śiva if one has been a follower of the doctrines of Vīraśaivism. This is called *śivācāra*. (2) The Vīraśaiva should worship Linga with a firm devotion. This is called *lingācāra*. (3) The devotee is expected to behave righteously (*sadācāra*) and should abstain from liquor and nonvegetarian food, violence to living beings, adultery, and theft. The devotee also is expected to be pure in thought, speech, and action; he or she should be charitable, and should always be prepared to sacrifice one's wealth, body, mind, and soul. (4) The devotee should follow an occupation or profession to maintain oneself and should serve the community. This is called *brityācāra*. (5) The devotee should always defend truth and religion. This is called *ganācāra*.

Righteous behavior (*sadācāra*) prohibits a Lingāyat from performing animal sacrifices and killing animals. Lingāyats should not believe in astrology, since they are beyond the influence of planetary powers. Lingāyats should comtemplate no other deity except Śiva. Furthermore, Lingāyats should not observe ritual pollutions arising from birth, death, and so forth, as they are consecrated by the Guru, Linga, and Jangama. Moreover, Lingāyats need not observe the ceremonies and obligations of caste and one's station in life.

Vīraśaivism allows equal religious rights to men, women, and children. A child, whether male or female, is invested with the Linga soon after birth. Widows have freedom to remarry. Virasaivism is open to followers of other religions to enter its fold if they take solemn vows to observe its doctrines. It is a religion that is democratic in spirit. It is monotheistic, believing in one God without a second. It prohibits idol worship. It asserts, with a single voice, the supremacy of God and the equality of all human beings. It promulgates the doctrine of redemption by the grace of God.

This doctrine finds a parallel in Christian theology. When a devotee repents for his sins and follows the path of righteousness, God certainly forgives him of his former sins. But the theory of atonement propounded by Christianity advances vicarious liablility. The son of God, Christ, was to use his birth in the world to take upon himself the sins of people. He had to bear the guilt of others, and was crucified in order to save others. It would be inappropriate to maintain an idea that a sinner would be saved without making any amends in his conduct. He would be absolutely free from all moral repsonsibility. According to Virasaivism, a person should shape and work out his/her own moral path with the help of a spiritual guide (*Guru*). If he stumbles in that path and commits any faults, he should sincerely repent for them and rectify them. Then, only, is he saved by God's grace, and not otherwise.

The doctrine of the Trinity in Christianity — Father (God), Son (Christ), and the Holy Spirit — has a parallel in Vīraśaivism. The idea of Father or God corresponds to Linga, Son to Guru, and the Holy Spirit to Jangama. Just as in Christianity, they are not three Gods but only one God; the same is true of Vīraśaivism — Guru, Linga, and Jangama are three aspects of one God.

The fundamental principles of Vīraśavia religion, in essence, include the following. First, God is one and He is Śiva the Almighty. Through His energy (*śakti*) He creates the world. Its philosophical position is that of energy-qualified-monism. This energy is constant, neither increasing nor diminishing. Second, matter is indestructible as it is created by God. So the world is real. Third, every devotee should aim at being united with God. Fourth, all Vīraśaivas are equal. Fifth, purity in thought, word, and deed are essential. Sixth, devotion, combined with knowledge (*jnāna*) and the proper action (*sat-karma*), are the means of approaching God. Seventh, every devotee should dedicate all possessions, including body, mind, and life, to God, the saints, and the community. This attitude is called self surrender (*dāsoham*). Eighth, egotism and all other evil tendencies must be banished from the mind. Senses are the root of all evils, and so the senses should be sublimated by investing each of them wih a Linga. Nineth, love toward God and all living beings is the basis of religion. Finally, souls are many, yet they arise from the same fountain head of God and ultimately merge in the same fountain.

These foregoing chapters, which delineate the fundamental religious-philosophical systems of the Vīraśaiva community, set the stage for a better understanding of the Vīraśaiva social system presented in Part II. The subsequent chapters demonstrate the symbiotic link between the Lingāyat religion and the community.

Emile Durkheim, the French sociologist, considered religion to be a social phenomenon. The Vīraśaiva religion, society, and culture are not only inextricably intertwined, but the religious ideals also present a unique synthesis of social and spiritual phenomena. At this stage it is useful to examine how the Vīraśaivas' religious values, norms, and beliefs bind them into a moral community and sustain their social institutions. A set of fundamental cultural mores have helped to maintain social control over individual behavior, provided individuals with emotional support, and have been a strong cohesive force in maintaining community identity and solidarity.

The prophet Basava, during the twelfth century, broke with an established traditional cultural order and provided a new model for a way of life that embodied a more rationalized and systematized cultural order based on democratic principles. This in turn had implications for the nature of the society in which it became institutionalized. In Part II we will begin with an overview of the life of Basava, his teachings, and efforts to build an egalitarian community of Vīraśaivas.

In the Vīraśaiva social system there are several distinctive stabilized patterns of interaction; some key interrelated social institutions; and clusters of institutional values, beliefs, roles, and rituals. The major components of the Vīraśaiva social structure and organization that are examined in Part II also include: (1) the monastic organization; (2) ideology and practice: social equality and inequality; (3) the socio-ethical codes of conduct and a paradigm of religious-spiritual values; (4) family and community; (5) the status and roles of women; and (6) the current state and future of the Vīraśaiva community in North America. We shall examine these aspects of the Virasaiva social system in the context of religious values and beliefs.

The Vīraśaiva social system and cultural complex provide a blend of social and spiritual values. The social order of the Lingāyats stresses that women have equal rights with men in social and spiritual spheres, and that there is no need to renounce the world in order to attain spiritual goals. Moreover, every Lingāyat is required to follow an occupation and share the fruits of one's labor with other members of the community. The social fabric, as manifested in the family, stratification structure, codes of conduct, women's roles, and community organizations, reveals the nexus between the Lingāyat ideology and practice, as well as their divergence. The sociological discourse that follows in Part II is intended to focus on the Vīraśaiva religion as both a social institution and lived experience.

Part II

THE SOCIAL SYSTEM AND CULTURAL DYNAMICS

8

THE SOCIAL VISION OF BASAVA

The Vīraśaiva revolutionary movement of the twelfth century in India, and its profound impact on religion and society in Karnatak and the surrounding regions, still remains largely unknown. This socio-religious reform movement was led by Basava, who is regarded as a prophet by his followers. The charismatic leadership of Basava, attracted numerous saints from many parts of India, from Kashmir in the north to the southern regions.

Basava was a philosopher-statesman as well as a social reformer and a rebel. He was a mystic and an independent thinker. Basava took the Divine message to every heart and hearth. More importantly, Basava is known as a saint-poet for his numerous devotional lyrics (*vacanas*) which profess a religion of humanity based on equality, freedom, justice, nonviolence and peace, compassion, the dignity of labor, and community service. His new religion embraced members of all castes and aimed at building an egalitarian community of devotees of Lord Śiva. This chapter presents an outline of the life of Basava and his contributions to religion and society.

Before we understand the social vision of Basava, it is necessary to know the nature of the society in medieval India that Basava attempted to change. The medieval society was based on a hierarchy of castes. The Brahmans formed the elite and enjoyed high social status, power, and privileges. The lower castes and untouchables were at a great disadvantage. They were discriminated against and exploited. The ideals embodied in the scriptures were rarely translated into action.

Furthermore, the religious behavior of the majority manifested a set of rituals and sacrifices. Their devotion to God seemed to be mainly a show for selfish interests without purity of mind. The upper caste members, who were rich and powerful, controlled the socio-economic and political institutions, including the temple. Women, being subordinate to men, were denied social and religious rights. Marriage at an early age was common. Remarriage of widows and divorcees was not allowed.

These conditions prevailed when Basava was born in 1106 A.D. in Karnatak, India. As a young boy he had to go through a brahmanical initiation ceremony.

However, he found the caste system and ritualism of his society unjust and meaningless. He went to a village called Sangama, where he found a Guru with whom he studied the Vedas and other religious texts and prepared himself to create a new community of Śiva's devotees, known as the Vīraśaiva or Lingāyata, disregarding the distinctions of caste, class, gender, and the orthodox rituals.

Later on, Basava went to the city of Kalyāna, where he was appointed minister to King Bijjala of the Kalachuri dynasty in Karnatak (Ishwaran, 1992). In Kalyāna, Basava established an academy called the Hall of Spiritual Experience (*Anubhava Mantapa*), which attracted numerous saints and spiritual aspirants from different parts of India.

The religion of Basava is monotheistic; it vehemently proclaims that Lord Śiva is the only Supreme Reality. Basava declared that the essence of religion implies living a life of goodness and humility based on a synthesis of right knowledge, deep devotion, and virtuous action. The egalitarian community of Basava stressed the purity of both body and mind.

Basava inspired people to live by a set of ethical norms and responsibilities and to follow a way of life governed by the moral principles of honesty, work (*Kāyaka*) dedicated to Śiva, frugality, sharing, and community service (*dāsoha*). The notion of God in Vīraśaivism denotes a dual commitment — the commitment to the doctrine of individual liberty and equality, and an equal commitment to the community and society.

Basava did not approve of either the worship of several gods or idolatry. He said, "God is but one, many His names." Basava clearly distinguished the religions based on fear and superstitions from the religion of love and selfless devotion. Basava maintained that prayers and meditation serve as a personal communion between the devotee and God. Basava upheld only the faith which aided spiritual pursuits and condemned blind beliefs and superstitious customs associated with stars, omens, the influence of auspicious and inauspicious time periods, pilgrimages to holy places for cleansing sins and attaining religious merit, and so forth. He gave the utmost importance to purity of thought and purity of action.

Basava considered the body of a devotee as a temple. He believed that God resides in one's own heart. "Make your body the temple of God," said Basava.

> The rich
> Will make temples for Śiva
> What shall I,
> a poor man, do?
> My legs are pillars,
> the body the shrine,
> the head the cupola of gold.
> Listen, O Lord:
> Standing things shall fall,
> that which moves shall stay.[37]

Basava mercilessly condemned deceit and theft, greed and violence, wickedness and unethical behavior, and gave priority to industriousness, unimpeachable character, politeness and sincerity.

Thou shalt not steal nor kill;
Nor speak a lie;
Be angry with no one,
Nor scorn another man;
Nor glory in thyself,
Nor others hold to blame
This is your inward purity;
This is your outward purity;
This is the way to win our Lord
Kūdala Sangama.[38]

Only when the devotee is pure in body and soul, can his/her devotion to God find fulfilment. The path of virtue is considered a necessity for those who seek liberation from the entanglements of this mundane world. Basava protested against the rituals prescribed in the Vedas (Murthy, 1972), but accepted the truth revealed in the Upanishads. Basava asked, "What sort of religion can it be without compassion?" He could not tolerate sacrificial rites involving animal slaughter.

The actions of Basava were deep-rooted in a sound philosophy and a noble attitude inspired by incomparable compassion for humanity. That is why he rejected the caste system and declared that a person should be judged not by birth, but by his/her thoughts, character, and behavior. This was indeed revolutionary in twelfth century India. Basava's primary goal was to reconstruct a society where all persons would have equal opportunities for religious pursuits and spiritual development, regardless of their caste, gender, or occupation.

With one stroke Basava achieved both social and religious equality and a spiritual regeneration of the masses. Basava was the champion of the poor and disadvantaged. He advocated equal rights for women. Basava boldly declared that men and women are equal, as the soul is neither male nor female. Women were encouraged to pursue their spiritual activities, take part in philosophical discussions, and express themselves through lyrics. There were a galaxy of female Vīraśaiva mystics during the twelfth century who freely expressed their ideas supporting or even disagreeing with their husbands. Family life was not considered to be a barrier to spiritual attainment. The divorce and remarriage of widows were permitted. Basava was indeed far ahead of his time in creating a casteless society based on gender equality.

The concept of honest labor (Kāyaka) dedicated to God and undertaken as a community service is another signal contribution of Basava. The principle of the dignity of labor, which is characteristic of the Vīraśaiva movement, requires that every person should be involved in honest dedicated work. The occupation should serve as an aid to raise divine consciousness, to realize God, to share with others, and to serve the community. Basava sought harmony between the material world of work and spiritual attainment

Basava insisted that everyone must work. Work is not only worship, but also heaven. Basava revolted against the principle of following a caste-based occupation, and accepted the democratic principle of the freedom of choice of an occupation based on individual skills and interests. He proclaimed that no occupation was superior or inferior. Work should be productive and useful for society. Moreover, work should not be considered merely as a means of livelihood. Honest dedicated work should be performed with absolute detachment and should meet the needs of both the individual and society. In other words, work in Vīraśaivism meant the dignity as well as the divinity of labor.

The earnings of the individual should not only satisfy one's basic material needs, but also promote spiritual progress; and they also should be utilized for the welfare of society. Accumulation of wealth was condemned by Basava. On the contrary, devotees were expected to share their meager earnings with other members of the community. Work, when undertaken in a spirit of dedication, unselfishness, and utter humility, becomes worship or heaven itself. The goal of the Vīraśaiva work ethic is the equitable distribution of work and also of wealth. This doctrine of honest work emancipated people from superstitions, restored their self-confidence and spirit of freedom, and made them self-reliant.

In addition to his unique achievement of creating a community based on the rejection of inequalities of every kind, and of ritualism and taboos, and a society that exalted work in the name of Lord Śiva, Basava has composed more than a thousand impassioned, striking, devotional lyrics (*vacanas*). These lyrics convey complex and abstract ideas in simple language.

Basava's lyrics are powerful and spontaneous outpourings with the intensity of heart-moving devotion, the luster of rare mystical experience, and the insight of exquisite meditation (Tipperudraswamy, 1975). They express the depth of his devotion to Lord Śiva, self-criticism, social criticism, inner conflicts, the principles of Vīraśaivism as a universal religion of humanity, and the rich and invigorating experience of life "here" and "hereafter." A few lyrics of Basava, presented here, convey the divine message.

> Before
>> your beard turns grey,
>> and wrinkles appear on your face:
> before
>> your body shrinks into a skeleton:
> before
>> the loss of all teeth,
>> the back bent,
>> and you are a burden to your kinsfolk:
> before
>> you brace your legs with hands
>> and lean heavily upon a staff
> before
>> the radiance of your youth fades
> before
>> you sense the stroke of death:
> Worship
>> Our Lord![39]

> You swagger upon an elephant,
> You groom yourself upon a horse,

You parade in saffron and in musk:
And yet, alas! O brother,
You are unaware of the Truth.
You forgot to sow the seed and
nurture the plant of Virtue!
Mounted upon the intoxicated elephant
Of your immense pride,
You are riding directly
Into the snare of Destiny!
Not knowing our Lord
You only qualify for hell![40]

Melt my mind and purge its stains,
Test it and in fire refine!
Hammer, so the hammer pains,
To pure gold this heart of mine![41]

When once the body belongs to Thee,
I have no body apart;
When once the mind is Your own,
I have no mind apart;
When once the wealth is Your own,
I have no wealth apart.
When once I know these three
Are Thine, is there for me
Another thought apart,
O Lord?[42]

In the new egalitarian Vīraśaiva community a wedding took place between two devotees; the bridegroom was a former untouchable and the bride an ex-Brahmin. The traditionalists were enraged as it was a terrible blow to the caste system. The king of Kalyāna executed the fathers of the bride and bridegroom. Basava, committed to nonviolence, was deeply distressed. He left Kalyāna and returned to Sangama, where he passed away in 1168 A.D.

His vision of a society based on the ideals of equality and justice, the dedication of work to both God and community, the sharing of resources, love, compassion, nonviolence and peace is still an elusive goal for our contemporary materialistic society. It was centuries later that Gurus Nanak and Kabir preached similar ideas and practices. Mahatma Gandhi remarked (1924) that what he was trying to do in India had in a way been done by Basava in the twelfth century.

In retrospect, what appears remarkable is the fact that Basava, with his charisma and organizational genius, could transform popular consciousness and mobilize people toward social change in the space of just one generation. Sir James Campbell (1918), while writing about Basava's social and religious reform movement, observed: "Neither social conferences held today in several parts of India nor Indian social reformers can improve upon the program that Basava sketched and boldly tried to work out in a large and comprehensive program of social reform. The present day social reformer in India is but speaking the language, and seeking to enforce the mind of Basava."

Basava's life was a rare mixture of an active social reformer and a private, contemplative religious thinker, poet, and philosopher. Basava touched the very life-pulse of the people, enriched the literary and mystic traditions of the land, and directed the aims and aspirations of the people toward an integrated vision of a wholesome social and spiritual way of life. Basava's social vision and his message could become a major force in reconstructing our contemporary world.

The twelfth century socio-religious academy established by Basava in Kalyāna gave an opportunity for several philosopher-saints to engage in free and open dialogues. How this democratic institution eventually became stratified and well established will be examined in the next chapter.

9

THE MONASTIC ORGANIZATION

It is the monastic organization that influences almost every aspect of community life. The Lingāyat monastic organization, known as the "Matha," is intended to serve as the nucleus of a myriad of religious, educational, cultural, and philanthropic activities. For centuries Lingāyat monasteries have been centers of religious learning and scholarship. In many communities monasteries propagated Lingāyat doctrines. Initially, monasteries were probably modeled on the *Anubhava Mantapa*, an academy where dialogues on various philosophical and social issues among Vīraśaiva saints took place during the twelfth century. Under the charismatic leadership of Basava, Cennabasava, Prabhu, and a host of other saints, it was a thriving democratic institution where innovative ideas, concepts, and theories were discussed and critically examined. The members of this academy were free thinkers and were not bound by traditional beliefs and superstitions.

It should be noted that the Lingāyat ascetics are not organized either around a central church or on the model of Hindu ascetic orders. In fact, the Lingāyat ideology does not prescribe celibacy or asceticism in order to attain spiritual goals. Family life is not considered to be a barrier to spiritual success. However, it seems that by the turn of the fifteenth century, Lingāyat asceticism and monastic networks became institutionalized. Over the centuries a hierarchy of monastic organization has evolved. There are five ancient monasteries (see Figure 9.1) of the Vīraśaiva apostles or Gurus: One is at Kedāra at the foot of the Himalayas, another at Kāsi (Vāranāsi), in Uttar Pradesh, the third at Ujjain in Karnatak, the fourth at Śriśaila in Andhra Pradesh, and the fifth at Bālehalli (Rambhāpuri) in Karnatak state. A sixth monastery was founded by Basava at Kalyāna in Karnatak, who appointed St. Prahbu as the first preceptor. This institution, known as the *Jagadguru Murughamath,* has its principal seat at Chitradurga. The Gurus of all six of these monasteries along with the Tontadarya monastery at Gadag, the monasteries at Siddaganga, Sirigere, Suttur, Dharwar, and the Murusavira monastery at Hubli, among several others, wield considerable influence over the community toward mantaining the tradition, prestige, and culture of the religion.

Figure 9.1
The Vīraśaiva Monastic Organization

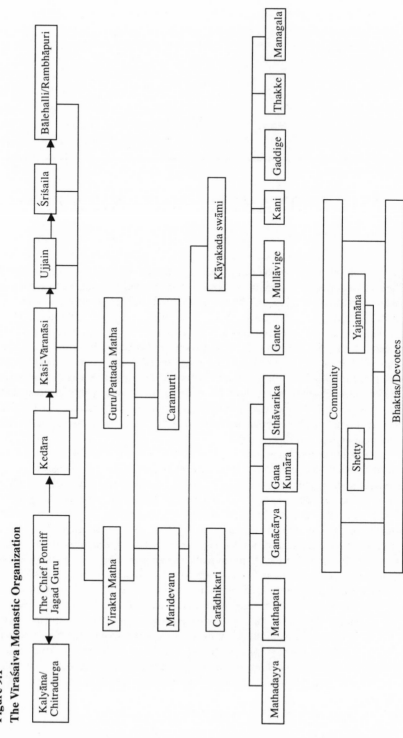

The Lingāyat monastic organization (see Figure 9.1) includes (a) the Virakta monastery and (b) the Guru monastery — celibate monks. In the Lingāyat tradition, the major monasteries claim to trace their lineage from the Five Prophets, or else from some linkage with Basava and his close circle. The Virakta monasteries were concerned with the liturgy, guidance, and counseling of the spiritual and moral lives of devotees. The Guru monasteries were entrusted with the task of interpreting and disseminating the Lingāyat doctrines to the populace.

With the passage of time, however, this division of functions gradually became blurred. Furthermore, the Vīraśaiva monastic organization manifested a hierarchy of monasteries, with the capital or main monastery endowed with the world preceptor (*Jagadguru*) at the apex of this pyramid (Bali, 1979). Every major monastery has a legendary saint considered to be its founder. The monastic activities center around the founder's tomb. The devotees are attracted toward the monastery primarily because of the extraordinary spiritual qualities and miracles attributed to the revered founder. The various branch monasteries, scattered over a large number of villages, towns, and cities, are at the lower echelon of this pyramid. The monastic hierarchy in the Lingāyat organization is limited, but nevertheless allows mobility of personnel.

The priestly class, known as "Jangamas," are closely associated with the monastic organization, but they do not technically form a part of it. The large majority of the members of the priestly class are householders. They can become celibates. In theory, monks can be recruited from any occupational group. In practice, however, an overwhelming majority of monks happen to be from the priestly class. The monastery-priestly class (*matha-jangama*) axis seems to have formed the nucleus of the organizational framework of the Vīraśaiva social movement during the thirteenth and fourteenth centuries.

The priestly class (*jangamas*) were assigned the responsibility of officiating at various life-cycle rituals and ceremonies, along with the tasks of the propagation and preservation of the Vīraśaiva religion and community cohesion. This monastery-priestly class organizational framework enabled the Lingāyats to have a sense of identity and solidarity, and to effectively confront the onslaughts of other religious communities. Over the centuries, this organizational structure has acquired a high degree of institutionalization.

The pattern of Lingāyat ecclesiastical structure, however, is different from the Christian church, in general, and the Roman Catholic church, in particular. There are a large number of Lingāyat monasteries scattered in different villages, towns, and cities of Karnatak and the adjacent provinces.

The relationship between the principal monastery and its branches, in reality, is not always based on a rigid hierarchy. "The general pattern of the Lingāyat monastic organization is not one of disciplined rigid organization but, rather, of considerable flexibility in a most decentralized structure or multiplicity of structures" (Oren, 1973:784).

For instance, it is the pontiff at the main monastery who usually appoints a person to be the head of a branch monastery. However, customs and precedents allow the incumbent head of a branch monastery to nominate his successor. In the event that the head of a branch monastery dies without naming a successor, it is also possible for some disciples, who act as trustees of the branch monastery, to appoint a successor.

Several Lingāyat monasteries possess valuable real estate in rural communities as well as in urban centers (Sadasivaiah, 1967). Donations from devotees to these monasteries help maintain various religious, educational, and cultural activities. Communication and interaction between the head of a monastery and his followers takes place in the form of attendance at religious festivals, fairs, and pilgrimages by devotees. The head of a monastery also makes annual visits to those villages and towns where his disciples are in large numbers.

Furthermore, communication and cooperation, indifference and controversy, or even conflict among heads of different monasteries is not uncommon. Nevertheless, the heads of the Lingāyat monasteries, in recent years, have felt the need to collectively deal with the problems facing the Lingāyat community; and they have organized (1994) the Federation of Vīraśaiva Monasteries in order to strengthen the comunity's solidarity.

The monastery-priestly class complex, by preserving and disseminating the Lingāyat ideology, provided a mooring for the social order. For centuries it has acted as a major institution of stability and continuity. In the twentieth century, Lingāyat monasteries, have been responsible for establishing numerous schools, colleges, and hostels for students in an effort to accelerate the spread of education, not only among Lingāyats but also throughout the entire region. Now monasteries are playing a dual role, combining both traditional and modern goals. The preexisting infrastructure has certainly aided the monasteries in assuming new roles and seeking new goals.

The Lingāyat monasteries have tried to exemplify active asceticism, on the one hand, and secular interests on the other. Although Lingāyat monasteries have lost much of their former authority and influence, they continue to be the loci of religious sentiment and cultural activities in the community. Thus, the Lingāyat monasteries, as important symbols of Lingāyat faith, still occupy a significant status and play a major role in the Lingāyat community. Of the priestly group (jangamas), the majority of them still engage in officiating at rituals and ceremonies. However, in recent decades there has been considerable occupational mobility among them. More importantly, many Lingāyat monasteries, in recent decades, have been instrumental in publishing and disseminating Vīraśaiva literature.

The priestly group seems to have established, over the centuries, an elite status on account of their knowledge of Lingāyat scriptures. Occupational differences in the course of time appear to have crystallized into status groups. The next chapter is devoted to an understanding of the evolutionary process of inequality and the emergence of caste/status groups within the Lingāyat community.

10

IDEOLOGY AND PRACTICE: SOCIAL EQUALITY AND INEQUALITY

The outstanding feature of the Vīraśaiva movement was its zeal for social reform. It rejected polytheism, fire and idol worship, the dichotomy of purity and pollution, caste distinctions, Vedic sacrifices, rituals and superstitions, the concepts of sacred space and time, pilgrimage, worship of God in the temple, and other traditional Hindu beliefs and customs. "The Vīraśaiva movement was a social upheaval by and for the poor, the low-caste, and the out-caste against the rich and the privileged; it was a rising of the unlettered against the literate pundit, flesh and blood against stone" (Ramanujan, 1973:21).

Monotheism, egalitarianism, the puritan work ethic, freedom, nonviolence, and humanism formed the fundamental basis that propelled this protest movement. These ideologies served as cohesive forces during the early phases of the Vīraśaiva movement. The charismatic leadership of Basava, along with a host of his colleagues, aimed at reconstructing society based on the principles of equality and the dignity of labor. Basava tried to evolve a self-sufficient casteless and classless society where everyone was expected to work for the welfare of society. Basava says, "Know what is good conduct and what is not. Difference of castes there is none." The Vīraśaiva saints were staunch advocates and sincere practitioners of these principles. During their own times they apparently did succeed in persuading a large number of people to follow these ideals. But, in subsequent centuries, the Lingāyat populace tended to be strongly influenced by traditional Hindu beliefs and practices. The Hindu practice of the worship of deities in temples, and the adoption of this practice by Lingāyats, demonstrates the consequence of the unyielding intermingling force of the majority of Hindus and the minority of Lingāyats. However, Śiva remains the central deity for Lingāyats; and the practice of wearing and worshipping Śivalinga (*istalinga*) by members of the Lingāyat community is still a striking feature.

The cultural ethos and social fabric of the contemporary Lingāyat is no doubt distinct compared to the Brahmanic Hindu social order. For instance, the factor of anti-pollution still occupies a central place in the Lingāyat ideology and practice. Their belief in Śiva as the supreme God is still undiminished. The Lingāyat kinship is bilateral. Women have equal rights and freedom in religious spheres. Divorce and remarriage of widows are allowed. These beliefs and practices of Lingāyats are in contradiction to the Brahmanical Hindu tradition. Likewise, various rites, rituals, and ceremonies related to birth, initiation, and marriage are also unique to the Lingāyats. The burial, instead of burning, of the dead and the absence of the ritual offerings to the dead (Srāddha) suggest that the Lingāyat ideology and practices, in their essentials at least, remain as distinct as ever. The common sharing of these beliefs and practices strengthens group identity and revitalizes the Lingāyat moral community.

This is not to say that Lingāyats in different regions of India are homogeneous. In reality, there are several caste-like status groups and social classes. Apart from the rural-urban differences and variations in life-style, beliefs and practices among Lingāyats can be observed. During the final decades of the nineteenth century, and during the early decades of this century, Brahmins and Lingāyats were competing for scarce resources such as education, jobs, power, and prestige. Some Lingāyats, on the one hand, tried to establish the antiquity of their religion, and attempted to show that they were in no way inferior to Brahmins by adopting some beliefs and customs of the Brahmins, including the caste (Varna system). The majority of the Lingāyats, however, maintained their distinct identity.

During the 1930s, for example, M. R. Sakhare (1978) noted that the Lingāyats of Maharashtra performed the "Srāddha" ceremony in honor of the dead. Furthermore, he observed different beliefs, customs, and practices among the Lingāyats in different parts of India. He found that the Lingāyats of the former Mysore State and Andhra Pradesh were somewhat similar to the Ārādhya Brahmins. A segment of the Lingāyat society, known as Ārādhya Vīraśaivas, performed ceremonies with Vedic hymns. The Lingāyats of northern (Bombay) Karnatak did not follow Brahmanic customs, and even today they maintain their distinct Lingāyat customs. The Lingāyats of northeastern (Hyderabad) Karnatak have customs that are somewhat distinct for that region. The Lingāyat ideals have served as important links between the past and present with the future. The fundamental ideals enjoy not only a large measure of relative autonomy, but also provide the Lingāyat society with a strong identity and dynamism.

In recent years, increasing levels of education and occupational and geographic mobility have contributed to significant changes in the attitudes, behavior, and life-styles of the Lingāyats. However, Lingāyat consciousness and identity seem to have been reinforced by many Lingāyat monastic organizations, educational institutions, and cultural associations.

While analyzing the interaction between religion and modernization, K. Ishwaran (1983) argues that the Lingāyats constitute a populistic community. Some of the essential features of this community include: cooperative interdependence of the groups, a significant degree of group pluralism, anti-elitism based on egalitarian goals, linkage with the external environment, and a built-in propensity to modernization. Furthermore, it is observed that the essence of the Lingāyat paradigm of modernization is the compatibility between the populistic community tradition and the universalistic model of modernization.

It is asserted that the Lingāyat religion played a role in the modernization process similar to that of the western Protestantism and its ethic. But it is maintained that they are qualitatively different because the Lingāyat work ethic (*Kāyaka*) and the Calvinist ideology of commitment to an occupation (*beruf*) and asceticism emphasize different goals. In contrast to Calvin's emphasis on the individual commitment to a "calling," Basava advocated toward building an egalitarian community based on the dignity of work, community service and sharing, diligence, thrift, and sobriety. Calvin's work ethic is said to have contributed to the development of a capitalist economy and society. Basava's notion of a puritan work ethic, in contrast, is aimed at a socialist and humanistic society.

The process of modernization among the Lingāyats has facilitated a high level of social mobility. During the past one hundred years, especially during the past four decades, Lingāyat religious and educational organizations have tended, by establishing numerous high schools, colleges, and free hostels for students, to reduce socio-economic inequalities. In recent decades, the Lingāyat community has provided considerable leadership not only in the field of education, but also in business and industry, and in politics and culture.

The Vīraśaiva movement initiated by Basava and his compeers during the twelfth century aimed at an egalitarian society where everyone, irrespective of age, gender, caste, class, or occupation, would be recognized as equal. The leaders of the Lingāyat movement preached and practiced the ideal of equality. In their view, the Lingāyat religious community should not be stratified on the basis of gender, age, heredity, occupation, caste, or on any other basis or ranking, because we are all created equal in the image of God. It is this ideal of equality that attracted thousands of lower caste members to the Lingāyat fold. The Lingāyat religious community grew rapidly and extensively not only during the twelfth century, but also in subsequent centuries. This growth was due primarily to its appeal to disadvantaged people in the lower echelons of the Hindu social order.

The Lingāyat society, during the twelfth century, was no doubt composed of numerous occupational groups. The functional division of society, however, did not constitute a social hierarchy, social differentiation, or a caste-based stratification as we know it today. The Lingāyat ideology of the work ethic strongly emphasized the dignity of labor. One's calling was conceived as heavenly bliss. No occupation was considered either superior or inferior, as long as it was performed as God's calling and met legitimate needs of the society. This revolutionary fervor of the Lingāyat society, without stratification based on caste or class, seems to have prevailed during the twelfth century and a few generations thereafter.

In the course of time, however, it appears that the traditional forces of the dominant Hindu social system again weakened the egalitarian social structure of the Lingāyats. Different occupational groups (see Table 10.1) tended to become endogamous groups. Over the centuries an informal system of social stratification has evolved, although in principle Lingāyatism rejects the Hindu caste system. Max Weber, Edgar Thurston, R. E. Enthoven, and J. H. Hutton consider the Lingāyats to be an illustration par excellence of a religious group that has become a caste or caste-sect. William McCormack suggests that the use of the term "sect" historically does not, however,

Table 10.1
Occupational/Status Groups

Priests	Merchants/Traders	Farmers	Artisans and Others	
Jangama	Banajiga	Ahir Lingāyat	Ambiga (Ferryman)	Lingāyat Badiger (Carpenter)
Aradhya	Badagalava	Gauda Lingāyat	Ganiga: (Oilpresser)	Lingāyat Baligar
Ayya	Bania Lingayata	Gauda mane	Dikavant Ganiga	Lingāyat Banakar
Chikkamatha	BannaDava	Gauliga	Dare Ganiga	Lingāyat Hugar (Florist)
Ganachari	Basale	Gurikara	Rasavant Ganiga	Lingāyat Kammar (Blacksmith)
Ganadhishvara Bavani		Gurusthala	Silavant Ganiga	Lingāyat Simpi (Tailor)
Hirematha	Gada Lingayata	Mallava	Jadar: (Weaver)	Nagalika Simpi
Hugara	Gaddigeyava	Monaba	Bile Jadar	Siva Simpi
Mathapati	Joti Banajiga	Panachachara Lingāyat	Kare Jadar	Mali
Pujari	Kaikola	Panchamasali Totiga	Koshtis (Hatkar)	Mochi (Samagara) (Shoemaker)
Sthavara	Kannadiga	Lingāyat Reddi:	Lingāyat Agasa (Washerman)	Nhavi/Nadig
Swami	Kanthapavade	Narada	Lingāyat Gauli (Milkman)	Neygi (Weaver):
	Korishetti	Pakanati	Lingāyat Jyandra	Bilimagga
	Linga Banajiga	Pasubumati	Lingāyat Kapu	Devanga
	Lokavanta Banajiga	Renati	Lingāyat Kumbara (Potter)	Medara (Basketmaker)
	Dhula (Mela) pavada	Yellamma Kapu	Lingāyat Kuruma	Sale:
	Nirumelina	Yellamma Reddi	Lingāyat Mangala	Pattusale
	Panchamasale Banajiga	Sadaru	Lingāyat Nayandar	Hadapada (Barber)
	Pattanashetti	Lingayat-Vokkaliga	Silavant Nayandar	
	Pavadashetti	Hande Kuruba	Lingāyat Panchalas	
	Petemane	Kuda-Vokkaliga	Lingāyat Madivala (Washermen)	
	Sheelavant Banajiga	Pakanaka Reddi		
	Togashetti			
	Turukane Banajiga			

rule out the fruitfulness of other approaches which recognize the status of the Lingāyats as a sect.

Max Weber noted that, in general, the Lingāyat, in accordance with the general fate of the sects, was once again pressed back into the caste order by the dominant Brahmanic Hindu cultural forces. In Weber's view, this evolution of a caste order took place in three ways. First, there developed an aristocracy of the sibs of the ancient believer over and against the newer converts. Second, status differentiation according to profession occurred. Third, the sect was organized simply according to the traditional castes.

During the first decade of the twentieth century, R. G. Bhandarkar (1913) observed that the true Lingāyats divided into four classes: (1) Jangamas or priests, (2) Silavants or pious, (3) Banajigas or traders, and (4) Panchamasalis. For R. E. Enthoven (1915), Lingāyats appear to consist of three groups of subdivisions: (i) Panchamasalis with full astāvarana rites. This subdivision includes priests and traders, considered to be the original converts, who could interdine and intermarry without restrictions. (ii) Non-Panchamasalis with astāvarana rites. This subdivision includes numerous functional groups such as weavers, oil pressers, dyers, cultivators, and the like. Each group is self contained in regard to marriage. (iii) Non-Panchamasalis without astāvarana rites. It contains washermen, barbers, and so on. Thurston (1909) quotes the Bombay Gazetteer (see Volumes on Bijapur and Dharwar) and repeats the same divisions presented by R. E. Enthoven. This division of the community into pure, affiliated and half Lingāyats is neither in accordance with the Lingāyat ideology, nor does it reflect contemporary reality. However, it is evident that conversions to the Lingāyat faith were made from various castes from time to time, so that the total number of endogamous status groups is large, leading to considerable complexity and fluidity.

While observing the social stratification system among the Lingāyats, we encounter the gap that exists between the Lingāyat religious ideology and practice. This problematic situation has been a matter of academic interest. We have already noted, that during the twelfth century, the Vīraśaiva movement rebelled against and rejected inequalities based on caste, gender, occupation, rank, and so on. The Vīraśaiva saints not only advocated, but also practiced, the Lingāyat ideology of equality, work ethic, nonviolence, freedom, and humanism. So, why, over the centuries, did the Lingāyat society develop certain features of the caste system?

The development of an elaborate hierarchy among the priestly class (jangamas), and the evolution of a caste hierarchy in the Lingāyat society, is attributed (Ishwaran 1983) to several forces at work since the late fourteenth century. The institution-alization of the Guru-Jangama statuses into the celibate and the householder taxonomies occurred during the fifteenth century. Subsequently, these statuses became hereditary. Likewise, other occupational groups tended to become castes and subcastes because of the strong and pervasive influence of the dominant Brahmanic Hindu caste order. Thus, the emergence of caste stratification among the Lingāyats can be linked to the predominant influence of the supremacy claimed by the priestly class (jangamas) and their vested interests to monopolize priestly and spiritual functions, as well as to the inescapable caste-oriented powerful Hindu social milieu.

The egalitarian ideology of the Lingāyats, although weakened, has not disappeared. It is necessary to underline the fact that the caste stratification among the Lingāyats hardly resembles the Hindu caste system. The Lingāyat social stratification is not rigidly structured. It is a more open, flexible order where social class status outweighs caste affiliation. The rules of connubium and commensality, which are so characteristic of the Hindu caste system, are not rigidly adhered to; there is considerable occupational mobility.

Therefore, the Lingāyat system of stratification differs in significant ways from the Hindu model of caste structure. The Lingāyat social structure is not based on membership by birth alone, but by conversion, training, and discipline. Despite a functional division of the Lingāyat society and occupational diversity, there seems to be no ideological or institutionalized basis for occupational or social inequality. On the contrary, an open casteclass system has facilitated increased educational and occupational mobility.

In the ritual hierarchy, however, the priestly class (*jangamas*) may claim for themselves the elite position. Although priests perform the rites and rituals associated with the life-cycle process, their occupation is not strictly confined to priestly functions. The Banajigas, for instance, who are involved in trade and business, have no doubt exercised considerable influence because of their wealth and power. The other occupational groups also have contributed their services to society. In other words, the diversity of occupational groups provides an integrated functional system for the Lingāyat society. In Weber's terms, these occupational groups in Lingāyat society could be described as a weakly knit aggregate of "status groups" that are partly closed but mostly open, and not caste groups in the traditional sense of the term.

During the early decades of the twentieth century, these occupational-status groups among the Lingāyats were endogamous and adhered to the rules of commensality and connubium. Since the 1950s, however, there has been a significant change insofar as the traditional status group identity and intergroup relationships are concerned.

The process of migration from rural to urban areas; increasing educational achievements and occupational mobility, and changes in the law, values, attitudes, and behavior have contributed to the erosion of the rules of commensality in urban communities whereas in rural areas these rules of behavior are seldom observed. Class status, rather than caste status, seems to be influential in urban life. During the past two decades, the rules of endogamy have not been followed by a significant number of individuals and families.

The patterns of continuity and change in the Lingāyat social structure demonstrate a considerable divergence between ideology and practice. The impact of the dominant Brahmanic Hindu culture on the Lingāyat social system is evident. However, in recent decades it seems that education and democratic values have once again been influential in weakening caste inequalities. Furthermore, the Lingāyat socio-ethical codes of conduct, which will be discussed in the next chapter, emphasize social equality, the work ethic, and righteous life-style for spiritual development.

11

THE SOCIO-ETHICAL CODES
OF CONDUCT

The social and religious lives of the Lingāyats are intricately interlocked. The commitments of family and society and the religious responsibilities are not compartmentalized. According to Nandimath (1979), to labor and serve their community is also an aspect of Lingāyat religious life. In fact, the daily work, family life, and spiritual endeavor of the Lingāyats are harmonized into the pilgrim's progress toward realization of the Supreme Spirit.

Max Weber (1968:19) has compared the Vīraśaiva work ethic to a similar kind of emphasis on the value of good, honest labor in Protestant Christianity. Although such comparison is warranted, a closer analysis has revealed (Michael, 1982) that the Vīraśaiva ethic of vocation is not exactly equivalent to the so-called "Protestant ethic," at least as that term was intended by Weber.

It is important to note that Vīraśaivism permits a choice of occupations based not on birth, but on interests and skills, and emphasizes that the primary path to eventual merger with God is through dedicated work and an honest and simple life. Excess gain from one's occupation is expected to be shared with the less fortunate members of the community. The Vīraśaiva concept of work (*Kāyaka*), or "calling," is based on the motto that "work is heaven itself"; it rejects a hierarchical occupational system based on birth, and accepts a more egalitarian social structure based on ethical behavior.

The Guru is extremely important in Vīraśaivism because the Supreme Spirit is represented in the form of a Guru. However, one who is engaged in work must even forget the Guru's sight. Even the Guru has to perform work pertaining to the socio-spiritual needs of the community. Every member of the Vīraśaiva community is expected to be engaged in labor. Even Lord Śiva cannot escape the law of *Kāyaka*.

Vīraśaivism attempts to bridge the dichotomy between world rejection and world affirmation by calling for ascetical discipline and self-control within the mundane world of work, family, and community (Michael, 1990). Ascetical self-control and spiritual development, through the pursuit of worldly occupation, is possible for lay men and women. In other words, Vīraśaivism recognizes work and worship as an integrated process. Therefore, Vīraśaivas are expected to carry on their earthly activities as divine service.

The Vīraśaiva social philosophy and world view (*weltenschauung*), as well as spiritual goals, are best represented in (a) the five socio-ethical codes of conduct, known as *Pancācāras*; (b) the eightfold shields or Aids for the devotees, known as *Astāvaranas*; and (c) and the six-stage system of spiritual evolution, known as *Śatsthalas*. These three form an integrated paradigm, the *summum bonum*, incorporating the sociological, psychological, and spiritual dimensions of Vīraśaivism. In other words, the Vīraśaiva religion as a set of symbols and norms acts as a "frame" for social action. The following analysis of this three-dimensional structure highlights some of the sociological implications of this fundamental Lingāyat system.

The five socio-ethical codes of conduct (see Figure 7.3) lay down the rules of behavior for Lingāyats as members of society. The first rule, known as *Sivācāra*, requires a Lingāyat to believe that Śiva is the Supreme Deity, the Absolute, the Ultimate Reality. The devotee (*Anga* or *Bhakta*), throughout his/her life, has to maintain the firm faith and belief that Śiva is the only Godhead to be the object of worship, to the exclusion of all other deities. Whatever devotional acts one performs, that is, prayers and thoughts, must be all about Śiva and none else. This socio-ethical code preaches social equality and religious democracy among the Vīraśaiva community members.

The second rule of conduct, known as *Lingācāra*, requires the worship of Śiva in the form of *Istalinga*, the amorphous representation or symbol of Śiva. The devotee is expected to wear the symbol of Supreme Reality on his/her person throughout his/her life. The Lingāyat religion is a pursuit that is characterized by a distinctive faith, path, and philosophy. In the later stages of spiritual life, the devotee proceeds to higher levels of worship, prayers, contemplation, and meditation of the Supreme Reality. In the advanced stages of meditation, the devotee concentrates on the abstract or formless form of the deity. Throughout one's life, however, the devotee should remain faithful to Linga. This socio-ethical code of conduct calls for strict devotion to Lord Śiva only, who is to be worshipped in the form of *Istalinga*.

The third rule of conduct, known as *Sadācāra*, demands that a Lingāyat follow a legitimate occupation or profession and strictly live a moral and virtuous life. The Lingāyat should lead a simple and modest life. Acquisition of material wealth is not considered a primary goal. A Lingāyat should contribute one's savings to the community for social, religious, and philanthropic activities. Everyone should be treated as equal members of society. Discrimination on the basis of occupation, gender, caste, or class is prohibited. This socio-ethical code of conduct also demands virtuous behavior, selfless work, and sharing with the less fortunate. Social interaction with other members of the community should be based on criteria such as character and the right moral and religious conduct of individuals.

The fourth rule of conduct, known as *Brityācāra*, refers to the devotee's attitude of complete humility towards Śiva. The Lingāyat is expected to maintain attitudes and feelings of humility toward the Guru, Linga, and Jangama. The Vīraśaiva saints have to be treated with all respect and humility. This socio-ethical code emphasizes offering service to the poor and the disadvantaged with modesty and humility. Furthermore, it is necessary to adopt the attitude of service and modesty toward all members of the community. In other words, as a member of society, a Lingāyat's social behavior should be one of humility, modesty, and respect for all living beings and should serve society so as to enhance the well-being of its members.

According to the fifth rule of conduct, known as *Ganācāra*, a Lingāyat should not tolerate scandal or slander of the Godhead and ill treatment of fellow members by anyone. This socio-ethical code expects every Lingāyat to fight against injustice, immorality, prejudice, and discrimination with courage and conviction. As a member of the community, one has to strive for its holistic development. These five codes of conduct are intended to cultivate among the Lingāyats a model personality endowed with the feelings and attitudes of devotion and godliness, fellowship, kindness, and humility toward all. It is expected that the Lingāyats, by leading a simple and honest life and by cooperating and helping other members, will contribute to community cohesion and solidarity. This code of conduct is aimed at the divinization of the Lingāyat social life. On this solid foundation is built the spiritual superstructure of the eightfold shields and six-stage system.

The eightfold shields, protective coverings or aids (see Figure 7.2) for the devotee, are a means of worship for the development of spiritual culture, and assist in the efforts toward the individual self's eventual union with the Universal Self. They protect the soul (*Anga*) from the onslaughts of worldly desires, evil thoughts, and behavior, and guide the Lingāyat to final beatitude. These eight aids include: preceptor (*Guru*), God (*Linga*), itinerant religious teacher (*Jangama*), holy water (*pādodaka*), consecrated food (*prasāda*), holy ash (*vibhuti*), rosary (*rudrāksi*), and sacred formula (*mantra*).

The spiritual preceptor (*Guru*) is one who initiates the novice into the spiritual knowledge and culture by investing the devotee with the *Istalinga* and by performing the initiation (*dīkṣa*) ceremony. The preceptor (*Guru*), who is well versed in Vīraśaiva philosophy and endowed with virtuous qualities, guides the devotee toward the attainment of spiritual goals. The preceptor (*Guru*) lives a simple, austere, and exemplary religious life, thereby becoming a role model for others to follow in spiritual discipline. Morever, the preceptor (*Guru*) is considered to be a manifestation of Śiva.

The prototype symbol of Siva (*Linga*) or, more specifically, *Istalinga*, is necessary for the devotee so that he/she may be imbued with deep reverence for the Godhead and impressed with the significance of spiritual discipline. The wearing and worshipping of *Istalinga* throughout one's life makes a Lingāyat conscious of the necessity of religious life and spiritual discipline. The *Istalinga* is not just a symbol of Śiva, but the Supreme Spirit, the creator of the Universe, and hence the object of deep contemplation. During the initial stage of the spiritual journey, the *Istalinga* is the object of worship and the devotee or soul (Anga) is the worshipper.

The itinerant religious teacher (*Jangama*), along with the Guru and Linga, is recognized as another manifestation of Śiva. The Jangama is an itinerant, moving from one community to another disseminating religious knowledge and guiding devotees in their spiritual endeavors. The Jangama, endowed with the knowledge of Vīraśaivism and tranquillity of mind, showers his infinite love of God on the devotees.

In Vīraśaivism, the Guru, Linga, and Jangama are recognized as a trinity that reflect the Ultimate Reality.

The holy water, known as *Pādodaka*, is intended to produce a psychological effect on the devotee with regard to the necessity of cleansing the impurities of the mind and cultivating a mental attitude of good sense and moral conduct. It is symbolical of the water of knowledge that washes away the taints of the body and mind, and serves to achieve the oneness of the preceptor and the devotee, who will try to imbibe noble thoughts.

Prasāda, or consecrated food, implies the favor or grace of God. By the grace of God, the devotee attains purity and equanimity of the mind and body. This, in turn, leads to the purity and freedom of the soul. The sociological significance of the holy water and consecrated food or grace was to remove all kinds of distinctions such as occupation, caste, class or gender, and to bring about equality in religion and society.

It is believed that *Vibhuti*, or the sacred ashes, will reduce to ashes anger, avarice, infatuation, arrogance, and hatred. It bestows prosperity, puts an end to calamities, protects one from the evil spirits, and helps burn the inward impurities. The *Rudrāksi*, or rosary, is considered to be a seed that is sacred to Śiva and a reminder of Śiva's steadfast yogic deep meditation. Its use in meditation and spiritual experience is considered important. The *Mantra*, or the sacred formula, refers to a set of syllables used for contemplation and meditation of Śiva. The recitation of this sacred formula enables the devotee to achieve the development of the individual self and its eventual merger with the Universal Self.

The sixfold metaphysical system (see Figure 7.1) known as the *Satsthala* provides a psychological framework for the devotee's spiritual journey. The individual self or soul (also known as *Jiva*) is male or female. This individual self wishes to be free from the miseries of mundane life and from the endless cycle of births and deaths. Every individual self is like the driver of the car of one's own life, so that one may avoid the ditches and pitfalls of ignorance and follow the righteous path to ever-enduring bliss. The individual self is made in the image of God, and it is endowed with limitless power of mind over body.

At the beginning of this journey there is a distinction between the devotee, or the individual soul or self (*Anga*), who is the worshipper, and the worshipped (*Linga*), that is, the Absolute or Universal Self. When the devotee, with the eight aids and adhering to the five codes of conduct, progresses in the spiritual pursuit, the distinction between the individual soul and the Universal Soul gradually disappears. Finally, the individual self becomes integrally united with the Universal Self. This process is divided into six stages, indicating the different phases of the pilgrim's progress.

In the first stage, known as *Bhakta sthala*, the devotee is required to offer his/her devotion to the *Istalinga*. In the second stage, known as *Mahesh sthala*, devotion gradually develops and the devotee has a firm and unflinching faith in *Istalinga*. In the third stage, by worshipping the Linga the devotee's impurities are eradicated, thereby obtaining the *prasāda* or grace. The devotee will pay undivided attention to the *Istalinga*. This stage is known as *prasādi sthala*.

In the fourth stage, the devotee withdraws his/her attention to direct it inwardly, and realizes that one's self is none other than the Universal Self. This stage, known as the *Prānalingi sthala*, is characterized by the inner experience of the self. In the fifth stage, known as *Śarana sthala*, the devotee progresses further and further and experiences within one's self the Divine Splendor. The devotee surrenders everything to the Linga, the Supreme Spirit, and enjoys pure delight.

The devotee (*Śarana*) is expected to lead a simple moral life based on purity in thought, word, and action. St. Cennabasava presents a description of devotees that conforms to the Vīraśaiva code of conduct.

> Dressed in the cloak of equality,
> With the cap of conscience on,
> Stepping into the shoes of passion,
> Without falling into the pit of darkness,
> Without being stung by the scorpion of pride,
> Without stumbling over the log
> Of renunciation on the way.[43]

In the final stage, known as *Aikya sthala*, the distinction between the individual soul and the Universal Soul disappears. The *Anga*, which is the individual self, technically merges and possesses all of the qualities of the *Linga*, or the Universal Self, that is, the Supreme Spirit. This ultimate union of the two is described as the state of unitive consciousness, beatitude, and supreme bliss. It is compared to a process of water merging with water, void merging with void, and so on.

Vīraśaivism attaches equal importance to devotion, knowledge, and action. The integral association of these three accelerates spiritual progress toward an integral oneness with God. There is no need to renounce the world to attain this unitive consciousness. What is expected is righteous and simple living, modesty, humility, and morality in all aspects of life. Social equality and spiritual freedom are not the privilege of a few, but are granted to everyone without distinctions of class, caste, gender, or age. St. Prabhu says:

> What means this young and old?
> In wisdom there is
> No difference in age.[44]

The work ethic and dignity of labor are part and parcel of this entire socio-religious and spiritual process that one has to undergo. In other words, Vīraśaivism tends to adopt the divine process of transforming the material world into God's grace.

The next two chapters on the Lingāyat family and community demonstrate how the Vīraśaiva religious values and cultural ethos have influenced the traditional and contemporary family life and community organization.

12

FAMILY AND COMMUNITY,
1880-1950

In advanced industrialized countries, in recent decades, falling birth rates and rising divorce rates, shrinking family size and increasing women's participation in the labor force; rising rates of teenage pregnancy, unwed mothers, and abortion; and an increasing proportion of single-parent families and nonmarital cohabitation or "living together" have been significant features of family life. In a world transformed by economy, education, and technology, the family, during the past one hundred years, undoubtedly has changed. These changes in familial institutions, however, have not been in the same direction or at the same rate everywhere. Contemporary global variations in marriage and family patterns continue to exist because of historical and cultural differences. Despite modernization and the consequent shift in focus from the larger kinship unit to the married couple and the emphasis on the conjugal relationship, in addition to the transformation of the family from a unit of production to a unit of consumption, some ethnic communities, in developing societies, have been able to blend both tradition and modernity in their family life. This and the next chapter on the Lingāyat family in India and North America are intended to present a contrast to the Western family system, and to identify those forces responsible for the pattern, rate, and direction of change characteristic of the contemporary Lingāyat family life. This study provides one example and attempts to show that the impact of modernization on marriage and family systems has not been the same for all societies and ethnic communities, as was assumed by Louis Wirth (1938), Talcott Parsons (1958), and William Goode (1963).

The family system is of paramount importance in the Lingāyat social structure. Familism is characteristic of Lingāyats. For more than eight centuries the Lingāyat family has been a major institution for the preservation and transmission of religious values and culture. The revolutionary ideology advocated and practiced by Basava (Ramanujan, 1973; Zvelebil, 1984; Ishwaran, 1992) and his associates during the twelfth century has had a significant impact on the Lingāyat family. The processes of modernization in recent decades have contributed to changes in traditional values and norms, family roles and behavior, intra- and intergenerational expectations, responsibilities, and relationships. Despite numerous historical and sociological forces of change over the centuries, the contemporary family still remains the citadel of Lingāyat religion and culture, and plays a seminal role in Lingāyat society.

There are more than ten million Lingāyats and probably more than four million Lingāyat households. Of the majority of Lingāyat families, about 90 percent are in the state of Karnatak, 8 percent in Maharashtra, and 2 percent in other parts of India; and abroad, primarily in North America. Thurston (1909: 260) wrote, "The Lingāyats number about two million." Referring to the 1901 Census, he adds, "These figures are of doubtful accuracy, and the probable strength of the community must be largely in excess of the figures." Enthoven (1915: 69) observed, "The Lingāyats are a religious community in India, numbering nearly three million at the Census of 1911, of whom more than half are found in the southern districts of the Bombay Presidency." In the former princely state of Mysore, at the Census of 1921, the Lingāyats numbered 714,734 as quoted in Iyer (1931: 87). We do not have accurate population statistics of the total Lingāyat population. The State's Reorganization Commission, Government of India (1955), estimated that the Lingāyats constitute 21 percent of the population of Karnatak. Considering the present population of Karnatak and the Lingāyat population in Maharashtra and elsewhere in India, my estimate of ten million Lingāyats appears to be realistic.

This chapter attempts to show the unique dynamics of the Lingāyat family system in the context of societal change. The detailed analysis presented here spans more than four generations and covers more than a century. For an understanding of the nature of the Lingāyat family in the final decades of the nineteenth century, we depend on the grandparents' narration of their childhood and adolescent experiences and the family life-styles of Lingāyats who are now in their eighties.

We have a few descriptive ethnographic accounts of the Lingāyat community. *The District Gazetteers* published by the British government contained descriptive accounts of Lingāyats. Ethnographic reports by C. P. Brown (1840b), Carr (1906), Thurston (1909), Artal (1909), Bhandarkar (1913), Enthoven (1915), Iyer (1931), and Hassan (1920) include information about the Lingāyat religion and community in the former Madras, Bombay, Mysore, and Hyderabad regions. They seldom present detailed and systematic demographic and sociological data. Since the 1920s, the Lingāyat religion, philosophy, and literature have received considerable attention by scholars. However, studies of the Lingāyat social system and, in particular, social institutions such as the Lingāyat family, from the sociological perspective, were not undertaken until recently. Since the 1960s there has been a gradual increase in the number of sociological studies of the Lingāyat religion and society. We shall review the contributions of foreign and indigenous scholars to the Vīraśaiva studies in Part III.

In addition to these sources of intergenerational, ethnographic, and historical data, the analyses of the Lingāyat family presented here are based upon research undertaken during the 1960s and 1970s. Discussion of the process of change in the Lingāyat family during the past four decades also is based upon the author's participatory and nonparticipatory observations of, and interaction with, a nonrandom sample of more than one hundred Lingāyat families in India and in North America.

It is difficult to delineate the complex regional, status group, and class variations of Lingāyat families. Such an analysis will have to wait for studies based on probability samples of Lingāyat households from different regions and socioeconomic strata. In the meantime, the present study intends to provide an overview of the structure and dynamics of the Lingāyat family without indicating regional or social class-based variations.

The present chapter addresses the issue of continuity in the process of family change. The specific focus is the relationship between the Lingāyat religious ideology and the family values and roles. We will focus upon the Lingāyat family transition within the context of societal transition from one generation to the next. As a prelude to a better understanding of the Lingāyat family structure and change, we shall begin with a brief discussion of the Lingāyat ideology. This will be followed by an extended analysis of "the traditional Lingāyat family" as it existed during the final decades of the nineteenth century and in the first four decades of the twentieth century. "The contemporary Lingāyat family" has been emerging since approximately the early 1950s. Although it is difficult to draw a clear-cut line of demarcation between the traditional and contemporary Lingāyat family, I would consider the 1940s to be a period of transition. The end of World War II and especially the national independence in 1947 have changed the nature, direction, quality, and rate of modernization in India. Hence the contemporary Lingāyat family can be identified as an institution characteristic of the past forty years. The manifestation of a combination of traditional and modern elements characteristic of the contemporary Lingāyat family in India up until the mid-1990s will be examined in Chapter 13. Also, some characteristics of the North American Lingāyat family will be analyzed within the context of the theories of modernization and family change.

In order to understand the complex interweaving of tradition and modernity in Lingāyat family life, it is necessary to take into account the Lingāyat revolutionary ideology as a starting point for viewing recent changes. The close linkage between the Lingāyat religion and family is significant.

The central values of the Lingāyat religion, as stated earlier, stress that this world is not an illusion. It is real because it is created by one God — Śiva, the Almighty. Every Lingāyat is expected to strive toward unity with God through purity in thought and word, combined with devotion, knowledge, and proper action (Yagati, 1943). For a Lingāyat there is no life after death. The notion of ritual pollution in cases of birth, menstruation, and death is alien to the Lingāyat culture. Dubois (1908:116) noted, "They (Lingāyats) do not observe the pollution periods of the Hindus, and their indifference to the ordinary Hindu purification ceremonies is notorious," and he quotes the proverb, "There is no river for a Lingāyat." Enthoven (1915:74) states, "Memorial ceremonies are contrary to Lingāyat tenets. The performance of Sraddha, or the funeral ceremonies common to other Hindus, is unknown" (see also Thurston, 1909:286-287). Thurston (1909:236-237) writes, "They (Lingāyats) declare that there is no need for sacrifices, penances, pilgrimages, or fasts. The cardinal principle of the faith is an unquestioning belief in the efficacy of the Lingam, the image that has always been regarded as symbolical of the God Śiva."

The seeds of modernity were sown during the twelfth century when the Lingāyat movement, led by Basava, challenged the caste hierarchy and ritualism of Hinduism. The Lingāyat ideology introduced a new social structure based on freedom, rationality, and humanism. The Lingāyat religious ideology encompasses the principles of individuality, equality, and fellowship. It rejects inequality based on gender, caste, or occupation. "According to Basava's teaching, all men are holy in proportion as they are temples of the great spirit; by birth all are equal; men are not superior to women. All the iron fetters of Brahmanical tyranny are, in fact, torn asunder, and the Lingāyat is to be allowed that freedom of individual action" (Thurston, 1909:249). In contrast to the subordinate position of women in the traditional Brahmanical system, Lingāyat women are accorded a status of equality with men. The Lingāyats are not prohibited from making a choice among a wide spectrum of occupations. There are no status distinctions based upon one's "calling."

The Lingāyat religious ideology emphasizes the cardinal principle: "To be at work is to attain bliss." A Lingāyat seriously engaged in an occupation is even allowed to forego the worship of God because work is considered heaven in this world. The Lingāyat work ethic does not view work purely as a means to obtain one's livelihood, but it includes a vital social goal as well. The fruits of one's labor are to be shared with others in the community. This is in contrast, for example, to the individual self-interest characteristic of the Protestant ethic. Furthermore, the Lingāyat ideology incorporates principles having to do with community sharing, diligence, thrift, sobriety, and nonviolence.

The egalitarian ideology of the Lingāyats challenged the traditional Hindu system based on inequality and superstition. The revolutionary movement sparked by Basava was instrumental in creating a fundamental structural change. Despite the weakening of its original rebellious force over the centuries, the Lingāyat cultural values and traditions, in their essentials, have persisted to trigger a process of modernization in recent decades. This process of modernization has been characteristically Lingāyat, precisely because the key terms of modernity are being translated into a specifically Lingāyat idiom (Ishwaran, 1983).

The Lingāyat family is an integral part of the Lingāyat cultural complex. It is shown (Ishwaran, 1983, 1992) that the Brahmanical Hindu culture is the foundation for the elitist *Mārga* cultural style in India, and that the Lingāyat culture constitutes the major source of populistic *Desi* challenge to this style. *Mārga* signifies an elitist minority cultural pattern while the *Desi* denotes a populistic culture. The *Mārga*, or the Great Tradition, is based on the Hindu Brahmanical Sanskrit tradition anchored in the Vedic texts. Its fundamentalist and orthodox position upholds the caste hierarchy, an elitist view of society, and pollution-purity rituals, and remains predominantly stable. Whereas the *Desi*, or populistic tradition, rejects inequality, elitism, and pollution-purity rituals, and advocates, in the language of the masses, an egalitarian society free from the distinctions of caste, gender, or class, and embodies an open, universalistic culture with a potential for innovative change. These two concepts help us understand the dynamics of the Lingāyat family system insofar as it manifests a selective blending of the *Mārga* as well as the *Desi* traditions, and a selective conflict between the two (Ishwaran, 1983). Furthermore, the process of modernization among the Lingāyats has been a unique intermixture of traditional and modern cultural elements. This study attempts to demonstrate this distinct characteristic change pattern of the Lingāyat family.

The symbiotic role of religion in the traditional Lingāyat family is still largely unexplored. The Lingāyat religious ideology extols family life. Married life is not considered to be a barrier to attaining the final stage of merger of one's self with God. The extended family was embedded in a wider kin network. The term "extended family" used in this study subsumes the concept of joint family. The pattern of multigenerational family living, the limited geographical dispersion of relatives, common economic activities, and, more importantly, religious values have contributed to a cohesive and integrated Lingāyat family. Enthoven (1915) states, "The greater number of them (Lingāyats) are either occupied in agriculture or are traders. The community may be described as steady and industrious, devoted to honest toil, whether in professional employment or occupied in trading or the cultivation of the soil" (see also Thurston, 1909:288). The rural Lingāyats today are known as good farmers, like the Ukrainians, Mennonites, and Hutterites of North America. The urban Lingāyats, like the Jews, are in business and professions.

Many children were desired on the grounds of religion and social status. Consequently, the Lingāyat family tended to be large. The average family consisted of five or more children. Religion played an important part in maintaining the family unit that included grandparents, uncles and aunts, and grandchildren.

In the Lingāyat community, the individual is recognized only as a member of the family. In the wider community, a Lingāyat is better known more by his/her family name rather than first name. In other words, the family, more than the individual, has been an important unit of Lingāyat society. What a Lingāyat does in the role of a family member underlies a Lingayat's behavior as a community member. In reality, the Lingāyat family provides the matrix for the development of a Lingāyat personality and influences one's life goals and behavior.

The Lingāyat home fostered the wholeness of life. It was the stage on which the drama of life unfolded. Home life included birth and socialization, prayers, reading religious texts and singing religious hymns, sickness and recovery, festivals and feasts, family quarrels, betrothal and weddings, and the serenity of old age and death. This family life experience had a major impact on one's personality and behavior. In sum, the Lingāyat family was an embodiment of the Lingāyat culture; it strove for continuity; it formed an integral part of the Lingāyat world view (*weltanschauung*).

The Lingāyat family values stressed the overriding welfare of the family, where the individual member was expected to make sacrifices for the good of the family unit. The individual potentialities and aspirations tended to manifest themselves within the family and community. A strong sense of belonging and identity with others in the family was characteristic of Lingāyats. A pooling of resources for the benefit of all and a strong sense of family pride prevailed. It was the responsibility of every family member to preserve and enhance their family honor. These values enabled the Lingāyat family to maintain its distinct socio-religious identity over the centuries.

The Lingāyat home was the scene of a series of socio-religious activities during the family life cycle. The family wielded a powerful influence on molding Lingāyat character through the inculcation of religious values. One of the major functions of the Lingāyat family was to perpetuate religious life. Since childhood, boys and girls were socialized in religious values and behavior. Each family had a family altar — a sacred place of worship. The priest (*jangam*) visited every Monday and on holy days. "It is a peculiarity amongst the Lingāyats that they esteem the Jangam or priest as superior even to the deity. They pay homage to the Jangam first, and to Śiva afterwards. The Jangam is regarded as an incarnation of the deity....The motto of the creed quoted by Mr. C. P. Brown is 'Guru, Linga, Jangam.' These three words express the Lingāyat faith, but in practice the Jangam is placed first, and, is worshipped as God upon earth. This practice of bathing the lingams in holy water is universal, and precedes each meal. The Jangam blesses the food in the name of Basava, and eats before the others can begin." Thurston stated: "Monday in every week is the Lingāyat Sunday, and is sacred to Śiva. This day is observed everywhere, and no Lingāyat will cultivate his field, or otherwise work his cattle on a Monday" (Thurston, 1909:280-281).

Children and adults frequently went to temples, monasteries (*Mathas*), and places of historic events associated with Lingāyat saints; they also listened to legends and sacred texts of the Lingāyat religion during the holy month of "*Srāvana*" — July and August. The recitation of "sayings" (*vacanas*), the reading-listening of stories of Lingāyat saints and religious texts, prayer and worship, singing devotional songs (*Bhajans*) in the family, and monasteries and temples — all tended to provide religious socialization to Lingāyat children, adolescents, and youth. In this way, strong religious beliefs and family solidarity were intertwined.

Traditionally the Lingāyat family has been a three generation family. Intergenerational communication and interaction manifested superordination and subordination. Parents were never addressed by their names; they were always addressed and referred to as "father" and "mother." The extended family tended to safeguard the family property and took care of the unemployed, the sick, the disabled, the widowed, and the aged. These extended families enjoyed power and prestige in the community because of the number of people and their economic strength.

The Lingāyat family life cycle begins with the matrimonial bond between the bride and the groom. Within the family circle the child learned the fundamentals of Lingāyat culture. Rites of passage (Enthoven, 1915:73-74; Thurston, 1909; Iyer, 1931:98-107; Nandimath, 1979:40-54), such as initiation at birth, naming, the ritual haircut, baptism, puberty rites for girls, engagement, weddings, and funerals, were occasions for orienting Lingāyats to their distinct customs. As the children grew they were exposed to Lingāyat religious literature and practices. While upon marriage daughters left the household, the sons' wives and their children were added to the family. The death of the family head was a major turning point, which normally resulted in brothers setting up separate households. This family life cycle was repeated generation after generation. During this process of fusion and fission of the Lingāyat family life cycle, the entire constellation of family relations underwent a gradual metamorphosis.

The sanctity of the institution of marriage was sustained. Every one was expected to marry, and family life was cherished. Marriages were arranged by parents and kin. The average age of marriage was around thirteen for girls and twenty for boys.

According to Enthoven (1915), "For a betrothal the bridegroom's family came to the bride's house on an auspicious day in company with a jangam" (see also Thurston, 1909:274-75).Though child marriages were not uncommon, consummation of marriage took place after puberty. Enthoven (1915) also writes: "Marriage is both infant and adult, sexual license is neither recognized nor tolerated, but is punished, if need be, by excommunication. Polygamy is permitted, but is usual only when the first wife fails to bear a son" (see also, Thurston, 1909:274; Iyer, 1931:92-97). Betrothals and wedding ceremonies were joyous family occasions for relatives to gather together and help one another, thereby reinforcing family solidarity.

There was close adherence to the rules of endogamy and exogamy. The Lingāyats preferred to marry a cross-cousin or an elder sister's daughter (for details refer to Chekki, 1974:80-83). The matrimonial negotiations were usually initiated by the bride's family. A pre-puberty marriage for a girl was the norm. Her unmarried state after puberty raised questions and doubts. The bride's health, character, social compatibility, and her family status were of prime consideration. Her physical traits and attractiveness were of lesser importance. The personal attributes of the groom, such as health, character, education, ability to work, and, more importantly, the socio-economic status of the family were closely evaluated. His physical appearance was not a major consideration either.

The Lingāyat religious tenets recognized that every day and moment are auspicious and that the life of a Lingāyat is blessed by Śiva's grace. However, many consulted astrologers, and the horoscopes of the couple were drawn to check the compatibility of the stars and determine the future well-being of the couple. Likewise, auspicious days and times were identified and adhered to at the time of weddings, important agricultural operations, new ventures, and major trips.

The Lingāyat wedding was filled with pomp and ceremony. A week-long wedding ceremony was not uncommon. "The marriage ceremony occupies from one to four days, according to circumstances" (Enthoven, 1915:73). Such a wedding involved great expenditure. The Presidential address to the All-India Veerashaiva Conference held in 1917 urged members of the Lingāyat community to reduce extravagant spending on wedding ceremonies. The family's resources were mobilized. The related family representatives not only attended the wedding, but also participated through services and gifts.

The custom of dowry among the middle- and upper-class families, and the custom of bride price among the working-class families, prevailed. In either case, the amount involved was small and nominal, and there was no pressure to pay a large sum. Divorce was allowed and remarriage was permitted, but such occurrences were infrequent. Enthoven (1915) observed that, "The remarriage of widows was one of the points on which Basava insisted, and was probably one of the biggest bones of contention with Brahmans. Among Lingāyats widow remarriage is common, and divorce is permissible" (see Thurston, 1909:278-79). Widowhood was not a major barrier in socio-religious activities.

The ideology of gender equality, in reality, tended to deviate in matters other than religion. The belief and practice that female members need care and protection by male members of the family was common. In the traditional Lingāyat family conformity to gender roles happened to be in accordance with social norms. Age and gender were important determinants of authority and status in the family. The division of labor and roles within the family also were based on gender differences. Men usually worked on the farm or they were engaged in a specific trade or occupation, and women worked at home: cooking, cleaning, raising children, and assisting in the family economic enterprise. There was a definite division of labor between the husband and the wife. Children helped with household chores, and, as they grew, they participated in family economic activity.

The father was the authoritarian figure in the family. He was entrusted with the responsibility of looking after the welfare of all of the members of the family. However, every member of the family was expected to protect and enhance the family "honor." The instrumental role of the father as a disciplinarian of children was recognized, but this authority was rarely abused. He commanded obedience and respect. The head of the family made major decisions that affected all of the members of the family. Despite his power and authority, in private the father did receive advice and counseling from the mother.

Women played an important role in the family's well-being. The equality of women in family affairs was recognized. In fact, women, in their own subtle ways, tried to dominate men, especially in matrimonial matters. Women have been the primary agents of the socialization of the children. Through word and conduct, mothers set an example for children to imbibe the Lingāyat religious heritage. Fathers were also responsible for the religious and moral education of children.

Children were loved and cared for by their parents, uncles and aunts, and grandparents. In turn, filial piety and support and care in old age were expected. Observance of ancestor worship was one of the main functions of the family. It emphasized the importance of elders, both dead and living, and reinforced family solidarity. The parent-child relationship was warm. Parents looked upon their children as blessings of God and as vital links in continuing the family name and heritage. These beliefs and sentiments were reflected in the custom of naming children.

The practice of naming children among the Lingāyats symbolized a close tie between the past and present generations. The naming habits reflected the cultural values and norms of the community. Personal names of children were usually those of their grandparents, which were the names of Śiva, Pārvati, Basava, Cennabasava, Siddharāma, Mahādevi, Neelāmbika, and Gangā devi. (For traditional naming patterns among Lingāyats, refer to Chekki, 1974:56; see also Thurston, 1909:262; Iyer, 1931:101-102). These names, being transmitted from generation to generation, have been characteristic of Lingāyat culture. These names reinforced family solidarity and community cohesion.

The husband-wife relationship was not based on love to begin with. They were supposed to develop love and intimacy after marriage. They did not address each other by name. The relationship between husband and wife tended to be formal in both the family and the community contexts. However, marital love and satisfaction were characteristic of the conjugal relationship. When the husband was not a forceful personality, the wife managed the household.

The mother was the key figure in the Lingāyat family constellation. She showered love and affection on all of her children. The mother, who constantly worked day and night for the welfare of her children and for her family's collective well-being, was a fountain of sacrifice and a source of strength and confidence. The sacrifices of the mother were acknowledged, and her sons supported her in her old age. The mother's expressive role was to give and not to receive. Under some circumstances, however, she accepted support from her sons with pride. The mother-child relationship, in many cases, was characterized by maternal overprotection. The children became the center of her life. She was proud of her children's achievements and lamented for their limitations, if any.

The mother-daughter relationship was close and intimate. The mother trained her daughter to be a good housewife. If the daughter failed to perform the required domestic tasks, or was unable to adjust to her husband's family, the mother was concerned that her daughter might bring a bad name to her parents. The mother was continually concerned about her daughter's happiness in her husband's family. Arrangements were made for the daughter's frequent visits to her parents. It was customary to deliver the first child, and also possibly the subsequent ones, in her parental home. Among Lingāyat families, parents often tend to have their daughter's children with them for schooling, holidays, and just to raise them out of affection. These daughter's children continue to stay in their maternal grandparent's family for months and years. Thurston (1909:263) reported that, "Tinduga or Tindodi is a nickname given to a daughter's son born and bred up in his maternal grandfather's house. The name signifies that the boy will someday quit the house and join his father's family, tindu meaning eating, and wodi, running away." Even today many parents have their daughter's children in their household for education, farming, or business.

The daughter carried fond memories of her childhood home and was proud of her parents and siblings. Emotional-sentimental ties among parents and daughters were often further reinforced by cross-cousin and uncle-niece marriages. The event of a daughter's departure from her parental home was filled with tears and sadness. Kannada folksongs depict a pathetic scene of a daughter's departure from her parental family, and the daughter's yearning for and praise of her family of orientation.

The father-son relationship was characterized by a certain degree of formality and distance. The fact that the father had to play the instrumental role of being the final authority and also be affectionate toward his sons tended to create an element of role strain. In contrast, the father-daughter relationship was one of love, affection, and tenderness.

The Lingāyat ideal of fraternal solidarity — that brothers should remain together in the parental household after they marry — was generally followed. Brothers shared in the family property, helped each other according to need and each according to his abilities. This ideal was followed while the father was alive and influential, although sibling solidarity tended to weaken after both parents were dead. However, brothers were still expected to help each other even if they did not live under the same roof.

The division of the family assets and the process of fission into smaller family units usually occurred after the death of the head of the family. The family partition occasionally led to fraternal tensions and conflicts. However, there was generally cooperation, mutual support, and solidarity among brothers.

Brother-sister ties were strong, and were continued throughout life. The sister visited her brother frequently, even after her marriage. Brothers and sisters met during the festivals of *Nāgapancami* and *Deepāvali*. The brother gave gifts to his sister and her children. He could marry his elder sister's daughter. The brother provided help and protection to his sister and her children.

The mother-in-law — daughter-in-law relationship was generally one of friction, conflict, and hostility. Initially, the daughter-in-law was submissive to the authority of the mother-in-law. Gradually, when she gained status and strength through child-bearing and increased knowledge of the husband's family, she became less complacent and more assertive of her rights. This would lead to frequent quarrels and emotional stress. Furthermore, usually the wives of brothers in an extended family did not get along well. Women's different values and interests tended to create rivalry, jealousy, and conflicts among wives of brothers on the one hand, and between mother-in-law and daughter-in-law on the other. This situation is aptly described in a Kannada proverb, "A thousand moustaches can live together, but not four breasts" (Mandelbaum, 1970:91).

The inheritance of property was patrilineal, sons had equal rights to a share in the parental property, with the youngest usually given a preferential choice in selecting his portion. Upon marriage a daughter received jewelry as her portion. The ornaments she received from her parental family constituted her personal property. As such, these valuables were of critical importance to her, especially in times of crisis.

The traditional Lingāyat family has been a closely knit social unit. It has been a miniature sanctuary. The Lingāyat religion not only extols family life and work as a prime virtue, but Lingāyat culture also revolves around family life and work. In Lingāyatism, as observed earlier, the central institution has always been the home. Religious and moral values were taught and practiced in the home. The home altar has been a sacred place for prayers, worship, naming, initiation, betrothal, and weddings. Holidays, fairs, festivals, weddings, and funerals brought the extended family together. Such family gatherings were highly meaningful, and these social interactions tended to reinforce family solidarity. Religiosity and family cohesiveness were inseparable. If we accept the proposition that, "the more positive interaction between family members, the more closely knit is the family," then the Lingāyat family formed a more closely knit family.

The traditional Lingāyat family, with its traditional system of marriage, immovable property holdings, and, above all, the Lingāyat religious values of collective sharing, was closely related to the peasant economy, and hence the Lingāyats formed a populistic community. These institutions and values have undergone some changes in the last few decades. The Karnatak society, composed of a majority of Lingāyats, has become more urbanized and industrialized since the early 1950s. Education and occupational mobility have influenced family life-styles. Women are more educated and marry at a later age than before. Since the late 1950s, the law of inheritance and succession has provided women with the right to a share in the ancestral property of the parental family and the property of the husband. The law of marriage allows divorce on certain grounds. With increasing exposure to modern science and technology and to urban values, it is difficult to imagine that the traditional

Lingāyat family system would remain intact. The available sociological data on the contemporary Lingāyat family tend to support the hypothesis that the family, in the process of change, has manifested a selective blend of traditional and modern elements.

13

CONTEMPORARY FAMILY AND COMMUNITY, 1951-1996

Let us turn now to an examination of the contemporary Lingāyat family. As a part of a major research project on the impact of modernization in the early 1960s, a study (Chekki, 1974) of the Lingāyat family and kinship was undertaken. The findings of this study help us to understand some crucial aspects of the Lingāyat family system. The contemporary Lingāyat family in the process of change exhibits a remarkable mosaic of tradition and modernity. Before venturing to make further generalizations, it is necessary to consider some distinct characteristics of the Lingāyat family and community under sociological observation.

A study of a sample of 115 Lingāyat households in a rural-urban fringe community that constituted a suburb of Dharwar city in North Karnatak shows that the Lingāyat family, while retaining the revolutionary ideology and traditional family life, has been integrating new cultural traits in its process of adaptation to modern conditions. Of the 115 households, 43 percent were composed of nuclear families, 37 percent of extended families, and 21 percent of neither nuclear nor extended families. The largest proportion (46 percent) of households included five to seven persons, followed by households with two to four persons. The heads of 58 percent of these families were engaged in farming, 34 percent were in the trades, professions, or service occupations, while 8 percent were senior citizens. 75 percent of these Lingāyat families belonged to the middleclass, 28 percent to the working class, and 12 percent to the upper class.

The coexistence of traditional and modern elements are characteristic of the Lingāyat family in that there are both nuclear and extended families interlinked in many ways. The Lingāyats have a great store of knowledge about their relatives. Women, in particular, tend to be the genealogical experts. Children have close, affectionate, and sentimental ties with the mother. The matricentered family ties are in contrast to a strong patrilateral orientation that is evident in the inheritance of property, patrilocal residence, and jural rights and obligations.

The Lingāyat family is strongly embedded in the wider extended family system. A large majority of families are interrelated and there is a high frequency of social interaction. They exchange services, gifts, and counseling during normal and difficult times. Mutual aid and cooperation are characteristic among families engaged in agriculture.

Ancestor worship and the naming habits of the Lingāyats reflect the continuing filial piety. The annual worship of ancestors is an important family festival. The celebration of this festival helps the family to transmit the image of their forefathers to the next generation and also reinforces family solidarity. Furthermore, the practice of naming children among the Lingāyats symbolizes the close ties that prevail between generations.

Although the eldest male is officially the head of the Lingāyat family, in practice, the chief male breadwinner exercises considerable authority. If the de jure and de facto heads are not the same, the latter consults the former when making important decisions. The mother or the eldest female member wields considerable influence in the domestic sphere. In almost all family affairs, the husbands consult their wives when making crucial decisions that affect family members. Although both the mother and father play a dominant role in the socialization of the child, the final authority to discipline the child rests with the father. Despite rivalry among brothers, which is usually expressed in the sharing of parental property, sibling bonds of affection continue even after marriage unless seriously undermined by jealous wives. The mother's brother has a special role in various rites of passage. Furthermore, he acts as a friend and guardian to his sister's children.

The mother is the most affectionate figure for children in the family. The mother controls the behavior of the children through reward and punishment, and consequently plays a dominant role in the socialization process of the child. An expressive role is characteristic of the wife-mother. The husband-father in the Lingāyat family plays an instrumental role.

The family of orientation and the family of procreation often reside in the same city, same suburb, or in the majority of cases, within a distance of approximately thirty miles. This geographical propinquity facilitates frequent interaction among relatives.

The traditional family norm is to respect the elders and to obey the parents. As perceived by senior citizens, there have been changes in filial piety, and youngsters pay only token respect to the old. This change is attributed to modern ideals of equality and individualism, and to factors such as modern education, movies, economic independence, and secularism. The younger generation, however, expresses the view that their grandparents are reluctant to adjust to the changing society.

The Lingāyats consider marriage to be a sacred union that forms a basis for the family life for everyone. In rural communities a large majority of marriages are still arranged by parents. In mate selection the rules of endogamy exert influence. The traditional preference for cross-cousin and uncle-niece marriages continues, albeit with lesser frequency in recent years.

Marriage is still considered to be a union of two families, rather than just a bond between two individuals. The interests of the married couple are expected to be subordinate to the common goals of the family. In this context, love between potential spouses does not precede marriage, but is supposed to develop after marriage.

In the selection of a bride, family traditions, socio-economic status, as well as the bride's character, age, health, education, and her capacity to adjust to the groom's family are prime considerations. In the selection of a bridegroom, besides the socio-economic status of the groom's family, the groom's health, education, and his earning capacity are the criteria used for evaluation. The high frequency of early marriages in the past indicated the need for marriages to be arranged by parents (Chekki, 1968; 1974). In recent decades, however, with an increase in the average age at first marriage, the traditional arranged marriage has come under attack.

In recent decades, the median age of marriage among Lingāyat girls has gone up and prepuberty marriages, if any, have become the exception. Today, the head of the Lingāyat family still has a major responsibility for arranging the marriage of children. Among the urban middle-class families, the task of finding a suitable bridegroom is all the more difficult. There are more college educated girls now than ever before. The premarital heterosexual social interaction is extremely limited. Dating and courtship practices are yet to develop.

In recent decades, the trends in mate selection suggest that the boy has a greater say in the selection of the girl, while the boy's family retains the right to approve or disapprove of the girl's family. While the older generation feels that the ideal mate for a man is his (elder) sister's daughter or a cross-cousin, the younger generation tends to avoid preferential kin marriages. In the past the custom of dowry was not a major financial burden since, in actuality, it was a token sum of money presented to the groom. In recent years, however, the dowry amount in the marriage market has soared to new heights, and the payment of the dowry has become a heavy financial burden for most middle-class families. In the absence of dating and courtship, the mate selection process is dependent on traditional matchmakers and informal networks of relatives and friends. The need for marriage counseling, dating, and family-life education is now being felt among urban Lingāyat families.

The Lingāyat ideology of gender equality is indicated by the fact that divorce and remarriage of divorcees and widows are allowed. My comparative study of the Lingāyat and Brahmin communities (1974) in Dharwar found fourteen cases of divorce and an equal number of remarriages of widows and divorcees among the Lingāyats, but none among the Brahmins. The attitudes of the Lingāyats were favorable toward divorce and remarriage, whereas a large majority of the Brahmans were against divorce and widow remarriages. The Lingāyat religious ideology rejected the male dominance characteristic of the Brahmanical tradition.

The structure of the farm families is closely related to occupation and use of the land. It is the farm family that is the basic unit of economic production. Agricultural operations require the cooperative effort of all members of the family. A large portion of the labor on farms is provided by the family. The absence of hired labor on most farms implies that every member of the family works very hard. The economic interdependence and the work ethic of the Lingāyat religion tend to reinforce family unity. Among the urban educated families, the occupational diversity is evident.

Where changes in the Lingāyat family system are concerned, the proportion of nuclear households tends to increase gradually over the generations. This is more evident among the urban Lingāyat families than among the rural Lingāyat families. The size of the family also has been shrinking. The circle of close relatives is more limited than before. Generation after generation, there has been a declining trend in the frequency of the exchange of services, mutual aid, and cooperation among relatives. Filial piety and respect for elders has been waning over the years.

A decline in the authority and decision-making power of the head of the extended family is inferred from such changes as the increase in the civil and legal rights of sons and daughters, the lessening control of parents in the choice of mates for their children, and the education and economic independence of children, associated with neolocal family life. In recent years, ancestor worship has assumed a degree of formality and simplicity. There has been a trend toward naming children along modern lines without an ancestral or religious basis. In urban communities, it appears that most are not willing to make sacrifices for any member of the extended group of relatives except their very close relatives. Besides the process of urbanization, industrialization, and the spread of modern education, the two World Wars, the Great Depression, and, more importantly, the national freedom movement led by Mahatma Gandhi during the 1920-1946 period have had a significant impact on the Lingāyat family. Many Lingāyats participated in the national freedom movement by sacrificing their jobs and family life.

The educational achievements of family members have lead to upward social mobility. During the last two decades of the nineteenth century a large majority of Lingāyats were either illiterate or had some elementary education. Thurston (1909:262) reported that "The Jangams are mostly literate, and the members of the Banajig or trader class are frequently literate. The other classes of men, and the women of all classes, are practically illiterate. In Bellary the teachers in several of the Board schools (primary standard) are Jangams. Very few Lingāyats have as yet completed for University honors, and the number of Lingāyat graduates is small." The first session of the All-India Veerashaiva Conference, held at Dharwar in 1904, addressed issues such as education, religious instruction, marriage, and other matters affecting the welfare of the Lingāyat community as a whole (see Thurston, 1909:253). The President of the All-India Veerashaiva Conference in 1917 stressed the need for education of boys and especially for girls.

The All India Vīraśaiva Conference, established in 1904, recognized the need for promoting education among the Lingāyats. The Mysore Lingāyat Education Fund Association (1905) encouraged Lingāyats to pursue postsecondary education by providing scholarships. A small group of enlightened Lingāyats established the Lingāyat Education Association as early as 1883 to support the Lingāyats in need who wished to pursue higher education in North Karnatak. In 1916, the Karnatak Lingāyat Education (K.L.E.) Society was formed and a number of high schools were established. This provided opportunities for many Lingāyats to receive a modern education. Up until 1917 there was not a single college in northern Karnatak. Therefore, Lingāyats had to go to Poona and Bombay for higher education in liberal arts, law, medicine, and engineering. During the last five decades, the K.L.E. Society has opened several arts, science, medicine, law, commerce, and engineering colleges in different parts of Karnatak. The proliferation of educational institutions, and the increasing aspirations for higher education, have contributed to a significant increase in the number of Lingāyat graduates. Modern postsecondary education is a major means of acquiring higher social status for the individual Lingāyat and the family. The achievement of a higher level of education has facilitated a greater degree of occupational and social mobility among Lingāyats. Moreover, modern education is an important factor in changing the traditional values and behavior of Lingāyats and their family life-styles.

Earlier we noted that the Lingāyat revolutionary ideology of equality, introduced in the twelfth century, allowed divorce and remarriage. Therefore, the Hindu Marriage Act, 1955, did not represent a radical piece of legislation for the Lingāyat. On the contrary, it reinforced the Lingāyat ideology of gender equality. The Lingāyats are patrilineal in terms of inheritance of property. The Hindu Succession Act, 1958, conferred on women the rights of succession and possession of property from the family of orientation. A woman's right to have a share in the parental property, granted by this legislation, is indeed another extension of the Lingāyat ideology of equality.

The married couple, widow, or widower without a son tend to adopt a close relative such as a daughter's or a brother's son. The motivating factors for adoption are the need for maintenance and care in old age, and the need to inherit the family property and perpetuate the family name. In the absence of parents, the eldest son has the responsibility of taking care of his younger brothers and sisters. He has to provide for their education, health care, and marriage, and assist them in securing jobs. Even the widowed sister takes refuge under the care of the brother. Such sibling solidarity is characteristic of Lingāyats.

Modern technology, education, the new values disseminated through the mass media, and the secular egalitarian state policies are influencing the younger generation of Lingāyats far more now than ever before. Agencies external to the family increasingly impinge on individual family members and instill in them new aspirations and ambitions. However, in the absence of adequate social security programs and social welfare services, the Lingāyat family still plays an important role in supporting its members in both normal and difficult times. The individual's economic dependence on the family is still great.

The process of modernization has accelerated since 1947. Through a series of national development plans, agricultural growth, industrialization, urbanization, education, and socio-legal reforms have received special attention. The process of modernization has not only increased in speed, but it has assumed a new direction and dimension.

The sociological literature on the relationship between the family and modernization suggests that the latter affects the former. Modern education and employment, increasing geographical and social mobility, and the new aspirations and values of individualism seem to have influenced the age of marriage, choice of mate, residential patterns, the authority structure, and the solidarity of the extended family. The sociological focus has shifted from the earlier examination of the disintegration of the extended/joint family to that of changes in family role perceptions, interpersonal relationships, and behavior.

Today, the Lingāyat family demonstrates the phenomena of both the changing and continuing norms, values, and behavior. The rules of endogamy are being ignored. The younger generation tends to be more achievement oriented, interested in the self rather than the extended family, and assertive of their individual rights. The differences in family values and behavior between generations are increasing. The generation gap, and the stresses and strains between generations, are often becoming issues of concern. The family and place of work are separated, removing the economic bonds of cohesion of the family.

The modern urban occupational structure demands persons with special training and skills not normally provided by the family. The differing family and economic roles tend to break the traditional association between the family and social status aspiration. The educational institutions and occupational organizations reward individual merit and performance. The intergenerational and intragenerational occupational mobility, which has been on the increase for the last four decades, usually does not facilitate joint economic enterprise among members of the extended family. However, there are several cases of joint economic enterprises in business and industry among urban Lingāyat families. Father-son, brother-brother, or even three-generation joint ventures are not uncommon.

In urban communities, Lingāyats are more exposed to new values and role models outside the family. Increasing social and geographical mobility, and neolocal residential patterns tend to reduce the immediate surveillance and control by parents. The patrilineal family system is becoming multilateral and radial in content. Social legislation (Chekki, 1969; 1974), social security programs, and other welfare services of the government seem to minimize the importance of the traditional role of the family. The process of modernization and change in the family system of Lingāyats tend to be correlated.

A high achievement motivation is characteristic of most Lingāyats. Aspirations to improve material conditions are quite strong. Among Lingāyats, more women are attending colleges and are working as professors, doctors, engineers, and lawyers. Attitudes toward family planning have been changing increasingly toward its adoption. Such psychic initiation and internalization of modern values have tremendous implications as far as the Lingāyat family is concerned. The size and composition of the family, family roles, interpersonal relationships, and values and behavior among members of the Lingāyat family have been undergoing changes.

The contemporary Lingāyat family is more democratic, more educated and mobile, and smaller in size. It is less likely to provide religious functions and to participate in Lingāyat festivals. The frequency of visits, mutual aid, and exchange of gifts and services among relatives is now less than in previous generations.

Today the Lingāyat family is less likely to view the father with fear and respect and more likely to have mates selected by the children instead of the parents. Youth are less reluctant to marry outside of their social class or religion. The younger generation is more likely to practice birth control and family planning.

In urban communities, inter-religious marriages have been increasing gradually in recent years. With education and modern values, the average age at marriage has been pushed upward. As a result, the arranged marriage, although still quite common, has undergone change. An exchange of photographs, the meeting of the boy and girl under the surveillance of elders, and formal or informal consent at least by the boy, and less frequently by the girl, are now considered desirable and even necessary before a decision is made. Among the educated urban families, parents may formalize a choice already made by the young son or daughter, but these are still exceptions.

The number of educated Lingāyat women has increased in recent years. The educated employed women find it difficult to carry out responsibilities both in the family and at work. The problem of unemployment among the educated young has increased family stresses and strains. Widowed mothers tend to live in the homes of their married sons or with their brothers, and sometimes with their daughters.

The contemporary Lingāyat family is more egalitarian in husband-wife relationships than the traditional family. It is child-centred, where the mother assumes the major responsibility for child-rearing and socialization because of the father's absence from the home and his preoccupation with his job. Even though the parental roles and responsibilities are different from what they were a few generations ago, the home remains the central institution in Lingāyat life, and the children are the center of attention and concern for their parents.

The educated Lingāyats establish a new home away from their parents' home, often because of job requirements. However, the educated Lingāyat youth in urban communities continue to help educate their brothers and sisters, aid in the family farming or business, facilitate medical care, and provide assistance in securing jobs for family members. In this way, the Lingāyat family that migrates to the city functions for the benefit of the entire family.

The Lingāyats possess a high degree of emotional involvement, an intense consciousness of solidarity, and a strong awareness of standards of obligations toward one's parents and the extended family. Today, an overwhelming majority of Lingāyats recognize the family as a repository of love, affection, and warmth par excellence. For Lingāyats, the family still provides economic and emotional security in a society that is becoming increasingly urbanized, bureaucratized, and complex. Despite changes, the Lingāyat family stands as a central pillar of strength and as a perennial source of the Lingāyat culture.

THE LINGĀYAT FAMILY AND COMMUNITY IN NORTH AMERICA

The Lingāyat family in North America provides another dimension of its dynamics in a different cultural context. Although a few Lingāyats, for the purpose of higher education, came to the United States as early as the 1930s, it was in the 1960s that a significant number migrated to the United States and Canada. This is a highly educated group of Lingāyats. An overwhelming majority of them are in occupations and professions such as physician-surgeon, engineer, university professor, and research scientist. Vīraśaivas are highly urbanized and tend to be overwhelmingly settled in major American and Canadian cities. They are not residentially concentrated in specific urban neighborhoods, but are scattered in different middle- and upper-income suburbs of metropolitan communities. They are more likely to be owners rather than renters of their homes.

The North American Vīraśaiva community is based on a network of interaction, community consciousness, and identity. This new community in North America, although small in population size, is solid in organizational structure. An incomplete directory of Lingāyats, published in 1980 by the Veerashaiva Samaja of North

America, listed 234 Lingāyat families spread over thirty states and five provinces. An analysis of residential patterns revealed that a large majority of Lingāyat families reside in the eastern part of North America (Kumbar, 1982). The geographical concentration of families is more in the northeastern states as compared to the southeastern states. A few families have settled in the western part of North America — primarily in California. New York state has the highest percentage of Lingāyat families in the United States, and Ontario has 69 percent of the Lingāyat families in Canada. The states of New York, Virginia, Ohio, Pennsylvania, Illinois, Michigan, and California have 61 percent of the American Lingāyat families. The remaining 39 percent of the families are distributed throughout twenty-four different states.

After a decade (1991) another incomplete directory of the Veerashaiva Samaja of North America indicated that more than 470 families were scattered in thirty-six states and six Canadian provinces. A recent (1997) directory of the Veerashaiva Samaja of North America includes almost 700 families in thirty-eight states and six Canadian provinces. These Lingāyat families are heavily concentrated in the states of California, Illinois, Maryland, New York, New Jersey, Michigan, Ohio and Virginia. In Canada, the province of Ontario has the majority of Lingāyat families. Obviously, more than a 50 percent increase in the number of Lingāyat families within a period of sixteen years seems to be remarkable. Whether this is due to an increase in population, immigration, or because of improved snowball enumeration is not quite clear. Even today, several Lingāyat families and individuals in North America still are not included in this directory of community members. It is probably because the present system of enumeration has its limitations in terms of a complete coverage of all Lingāyats.

Among the immigrant groups in North America, Lingāyats form a rather unique ethnic community. They are a small minority, well educated, with a high percentage in the professions, and they live in urban centers. North American Lingāyat families tend to be small. They, like the Jews, value education highly. There is a strong bond of unity among members of the family. Every effort is made by parents and children alike to achieve the best in life. The high achievement orientation of Lingāyats is manifested by their high educational and economic levels.

Parents sacrifice their own energy, wealth, time, and comfort for the benefit of their children. Children are expected to be obedient, respectful, and loving towards their parents and to bring them joy and happiness through their achievements. Parents expect their children to be "good Lingāyats" and good members of society.

Both family and community life are characterized by a balance between the values of individual achievement and collective responsibility. The Lingāyat family in North America continues to provide the solidary base for the most enduring human relationship, as well as the nexus for the web of kinship forged by its members in India as well as in North America. Many Lingāyat family members continue to support their parents and/or brothers in India for improvements in farming and business, or for education and health care, as well as in times of crisis. This interaction and help reinforces bonds of kinship between Lingāyat families in India and North America.

The contemporary Lingāyat family in North America is future oriented and child oriented. It is far more democratic and egalitarian than the traditional family. The atmosphere of the home tends to be liberal. Children indicate their interests and career goals, and it is believed to be the parents' responsibility to help them achieve those goals. In the traditional family, the task of religious socialization of the children was primarily assumed by the mother. She was the preserver and transmitter of the Lingāyat tradition. She was expected to provide the link, for the child, with the total Lingāyat institutional complex. But the Lingāyat mother in North America does not seem to be adequately prepared for this task. However, her involvement in recent years in the socio-religious organization and her exposure to religious literature seems to provide her with some experience in preparing for this role.

Women are primarily instrumental in celebrating religious festivals, observing dietary rules, and in encouraging the children to engage in prayers. The major factor underlying the decline in religiosity among both parents and children in North America is the inadequacy of their religious socialization and knowledge of the basic religious texts, and a lack of observance of the Lingāyat religious precepts.

Although a few Lingāyat men have married across religion and race, in such cases their wives were initiated into the Lingāyat faith. Parents are concerned about the increasing possibility of the marriage of their children to non-Lingāyats. Conscious efforts are being made by parents to facilitate the selection of bride/groom from within the Lingāyat community.

The typical North American Lingāyat family is essentially nuclear, and the average size of the family is small when compared to the Lingāyat family in India. During the past two decades, the immigrant Lingāyat families in North America have been undergoing a process of assimilation. This is quite evident, especially among children born and/or raised in North America. The children tend to conform to the values and behaviors that are characteristic of the North American society. The school, peer groups, and mass media play an important part in the socialization process. The Lingāyat parents, however, make conscious efforts to instill in them a sense of Lingāyat identity through exposure to religious literature and family religious activities.

The children, as the first generation of North American Lingāyats, have lost their parental language. A majority of the parents, and almost all of the children, have changed their diet from that prescribed by the religion. Out of 106 names of children listed in the directory of the Veerashaiva Samaja of North America (1980), only ten names of children represent Lingāyat culture, while a large majority have a secular and modern orientation. The children have tenuous relationships, if any, with their grandparents in India because of distance and infrequent contacts. The younger generation seems to have more of a tourist's interest in visiting India, while their parents have sentimental ties with their own parents and other relatives. While in India for a visit, children often will persuade their parents to return "back to home," that is, to America, as early as possible.

The process of religious socialization of children that is characteristic of Lingāyat families in India is not so strong among North American Lingāyat families. This is because of the small size of the Lingāyat community, whose members are scattered among different parts of an advanced urban-industrial society. As far as the younger generation is concerned, the process of assimilation eventually may lead to a loss of cultural identity. Therefore, in 1978 the Lingāyats established an association known as the Veerashaiva Samaja of North America (VSNA) to preserve and enhance Lingāyat religion and culture and to promote cultural exchange between the peoples of the United States, Canada, and India. It is of interest to note that a similar organization of Vīraśaivas emerged in the late 1980s in the United Kingdom, where one hundred Lingāyat families are reported to be members of the Veerashaiva Samaja of U.K. The VSNA has local chapters not only in cities such as Chicago, Detroit, Los Angeles, Pittsburgh, Toronto, Baltimore, New York, and Washington, D.C., but also in the states of Georgia, Maryland, North Carolina, Alabama, Ohio, Texas, Tennessee and West Virginia. A high percentage of Vīraśaivas are members of the VSNA, and they actively volunteer for the organized Vīraśaiva community. During the past twenty years the Association has held a series of annual conventions, youth camps and forums, children's workshops, and religio-cultural competitions; has celebrated Lingāyat festivals; and has served as an important medium of communication for Lingāyat families in North America. From time to time, the Association has invited guests, specialists in Lingāyatism, and pontiffs of major monasteries from India. For the younger generation of Lingāyats, tours have been organized for them to visit India's historical places. Through its periodical publications, religious literature is being disseminated. One of the latent functions of the Association is that it acts as a marriage bureau. More importantly, it stresses the responsibilities of being a better Lingāyat in North America. In other words, the Association has been working hard to build a strong and cohesive Lingāyat community and a solid family based on Lingāyat religious ideology.

Intergenerational communication often does not seem to occur on the same wavelength. The relationships between parents and youth seem to manifest some degree of tension regarding conformity to religious norms, dating, and the choice of marital partners. It is not uncommon to encounter disagreements and conflicts between parents and daughters over freedom of movement and autonomy in making decisions. The teenagers who are exposed to the mainstream North American culture find it hard to adhere to the core values of their ethnic culture.

Although there is a sex-linked division of labor within the household, the gender role relationships among the younger generation have been undergoing change. The number of dual-earner families have increased in recent years. Both husbands and wives seem to participate in major decision-making processes. The dominant patriarchal authority pattern appears to have weakened.

In recent years, the Vīraśaiva Samaja of North America's annual conventions have organized special seminars, workshops, and open forums to discuss various issues encountered by youth in their religious socialization and cultural identity. Discussions have centered around themes such as dating and marriage, interpersonal relationships, youth involvement in Vīraśaiva organizational activities, teaching children and youth about Vīraśaiva religion and philosophy, and so forth.

The young Vīraśaivas have been publishing their own newsletter, entitled the *Voice of a New Generation.* One youth (Mahant, 1989:1) expressed that "most Virasaiva youth in North America seem to have no interest in Lingāyatism and do not follow the basic rituals." Most of them seem to attend the convention primarily because either they wish to "meet some awesome looking girl or boy or their parents force them to go."

Another youth felt disappointment and frustration because "the older generation seem unable to make a successful transition from the oxcart to the oldsmobile." The younger generation fare both cultural and generation gaps, and find it difficult to adapt to the best of both worlds, as expected by their parents. The apathy and indifference among youth can be overcome if parents, who are proud of their children's achievements, explain the rationale of religious values, beliefs, and practices.

Educational achievement and the aspirations for occupational mobility of Vīraśaiva children and youth contribute to a greater degree of their assimilation into the mainstream American life-style. They are caught between the Vīraśaiva family values and the American culture. For many youths it is difficult, if not impossible, to maintain a balance or equanimity between these two different cultures. Many parents, however, seem to be concerned about their children's apathy toward Vīraśaiva values and culture and their marginal interest in their religion.

The president of the Veerashaiva Samaja of North America expressed (Hulbanni, 1990:3) his regrets about the lack of communication with youth, and advised young people to read the religious literature and understand it before arguing against it. Furthermore, he reminded youth that "religion is not a science which can be demonstrated. Religion is a matter of faith and philosophy which can only be experienced not exhibited."

The Veerashaiva Samaja of North America has recently (1994) established the Hall of Spiritual Experience *(Anubhava Mantapa)*. It is situated in the Catskill mountains, occupying more than eleven acres of land, in the state of New York. This institution is expected to serve as a retreat for North American Vīraśaivas for spiritual contemplation and dialogues.

The foregoing analysis of the North American Lingāyat family and community seems to demonstrate a communication gap between the older and younger generations in terms of religious values and behavior. In the context of these unique patterns of continuity and change characteristic of the Lingāyat family and community in India and in North America, let us review the impact of the process of modernization in different national and cultural contexts.

Based on a study of family systems around the world, William Goode (1963) observed that the ideal type of conjugal family will emerge everywhere. Louis Wirth (1938) and Talcott Parsons (1958) observed that the extended family has disintegrated, and the nuclear family is becoming an isolated unit in urban industrial societies. Our study of the Lingāyat family in India, however, suggests that despite modernization and change, the family, far from being isolated and atomized, tends to be organically fused with the wider network of relatives. Many traditional Lingāyat values, norms, and behavior patterns related to the family still persist.

Compared to family systems in Western societies, the Lingāyat family in India maintains close ties not only with parents, siblings, and in-laws, but also with uncles and aunts, grandparents, and cousins. The rights and reciprocal obligations enjoined by the Lingāyat religion and custom are not discarded. A high frequency of mutual visits, and the exchange of services and gifts among interrelated families, is still evident. Even today, a significant amount of mutual aid and cooperation, communication, and consultation illustrates the symbiotic relationship between the nuclear and extended families.

Ancestor worship and filial piety still cement the present generation with the past and nurture the link with the future. The custom of naming children after their ancestors and Lingāyat saints is an important factor in fostering family solidarity and religious identity. Arranged marriages, endogamy, cross-cousin marriage, divorce and remarriage, customary laws of inheritance, and egalitarian religious ideology seem to present the Lingāyat family as a complex and unique system.

The urban Lingāyat family functions to preserve and enhance the family status. Both in normal and in difficult times, making sacrifices and helping relatives still are considered moral obligations. In the absence of adequate social security programs, the major responsibility of caring for and maintaining the aged, the sick, the unemployed, widows, and the infirm still rests on the family. It is remarkable that an overwhelming majority voluntarily perform these family obligations. This principle of reciprocity in action among relatives strengthens family cohesion.

In the process of modernization, the Lingāyat family is being transformed, but it has withstood the test of social change. The family has been adapting itself to the changing social structure. The contemporary family, as opposed to the traditional extended family, does not demand geographical propinquity and occupational dependence, or a hierarchical authority structure, for its viability. The modern ideal Lingāyat family type is based on affectionate ties and considerable mutual aid, and aims to facilitate the mobility strivings of its component member families and individuals. In this sense, the Lingāyat nuclear family does not face the world as an isolated unit.

A large majority still consider the extended family as the ideal. In reality, however, despite geographic and social mobility, and neolocal nuclear residential patterns, the extended family roles and relationships are alive and well among the Lingāyats. The contemporary extended family has not become atrophied. It is definitely undergoing modification and change in response to the process of modernization, and has been adapting itself to meet the new demands and expectations. The adaptive process is a selective blending of traditional religious and modern secular elements. The adaptive process of the traditional extended family is well described by Milton Singer (1972). He shows how the joint family system is not incompatible with modernization. In fact, the extended family system offers some distinct advantages for modernizing the Lingāyat family economy. It provides a nucleus of capital to be used for the technical and specialized education of its members, for starting new ventures, and for operating or expanding existing industries. There seems to be a striking coordination of tradition and modernity in the Lingāyat family system.

The pattern and consequences of modernization have not been universal. The different sociocultural systems have demonstrated the differential impacts of modernization. The contemporary Lingāyat family presents a distinct example. The belief that the traditional Lingāyat family has remained stable is a myth. For the past several centuries, there has been a gradual change in the Lingāyat family. During the past one hundred years, especially during the last three decades, the rate of family change has increased significantly.

Our study refutes a linear theory of social change and shows that traditional and modern cultural elements can coexist, as in the case of the Lingāyat family. This process of family modernization encompasses a selective blend and/or conflict between *Mārga* and *Desi*, on the one hand, and endogenous and exogenous cultures on the other. Far from being mutually exclusive and conflicting systems, tradition and modernity often seem to be mutually reinforcing. The fusion of traditional and modern values and behavior, without significant tensions and conflicts, makes us realize the fact that modernizing processes need not necessarily always weaken or destroy traditions. The Lingāyats have not been traditionalists. The distinction between "tradition" and "traditionalism" is important. "Tradition" refers to the beliefs and practices handed down from the past; as a community reinterprets its past, its traditions change. In contrast, "traditionalism" glorifies past beliefs and practices as unchangeable. Traditionalists perceive tradition as static; they blindly follow customs and traditions and do things as they have been done before. The ideology of traditionalism is antithetical to innovations and hostile to modernization; whereas traditions, which are constantly subject to reinterpretation and modification, constitute no such barrier. In this sense the Lingāyats have sought to reinterpret their past so as to make it congruent with their efforts to modernize.

On the contrary, they have reinterpreted Lingāyat traditions and have used them in adapting to the process of modernization and change. The process of family change depends upon and frequently finds structural support from tradition. In this intricate process of change, both traditional and modern values seem to impinge on the family and undergo transformation. Our study reveals that the contemporary Lingāyat family system incorporates the religious ideology, traditions of *Desi*, as well as modern values and behavior.

Max Weber (1968) described Hinduism as an impediment to modernization in India. Recent studies of the relationship of religion and modernization (refer to Singer, 1972; Chekki, 1974; Ishwaran, 1977, 1983) suggest that the relation of "ascetic Protestantism" to early industrialism, far from being an exception, may turn out to be one of the many cases of mutual interaction and adaptation between religious and social change. Lingāyatism, along with Jainism, Sikhism, and the religion of Japan (Kumagai, 1986) provide good examples of the active role of religion in facilitating the process of modernization. In the process of adaptation to different cultural milieu, the North American Lingāyat family has undergone significant changes. Nevertheless, it tends to retain some of the core values of the Lingāyat culture.

The foregoing analyses demonstrate the complex interplay of traditional and modern cultural elements and their impact on the family. During the past one hundred years the Lingāyat family has manifested a resilient ability to adhere to the religious ideology, while at the same time absorbing and blending modern values and behavior. The Lingāyat family system presents a distinct model of a unique intermixture of tradition and modernity.

From the oil lamp to the electric light, from the bullock cart to the automobile, from the wooden plough to mechanized farming, from oral traditions to satellite communication and computers, the Lingāyat family has come a long way. Despite modernization and change, the family has been tenacious to the essentials of Lingāyat culture. As in preceding centuries, the Lingāyat family appears to be capable of facing the challenges of the twenty-first century.

The next chapter is devoted to an understanding of the status and roles of women in traditional and contemporary Lingāyat societies.

14

THE STATUS AND
ROLES OF WOMEN

The movement for the emancipation of women in the industrialized Western countries has been a relatively recent phenomenon. The origins of contemporary liberal feminism are traced back to the eighteenth century Age of Enlightenment in western Europe. Mary Wollstonecraft's essay, "A Vindication of the Rights of Women," and John Stuart Mill's, "The Subjection of Women," both published in Britain in the eighteenth and nineteenth centuries, are considered to be the philosophical backbone of liberal feminist politics. The contemporary feminist movement is still struggling to establish equal rights for women.

In India, the traditional Hindu system recognizes women as dependent persons and undermines their personal interests and aspirations. Women are expected to sacrifice their lives for the good of their husbands' and children's well-being and success. Despite changes in education and the economy, and laws that have contributed to some improvement in the status of educated women in urban India during the past four decades, an overwhelming majority of women in rural India still suffer from inequality and injustice because of the patriarchal ideology that dominates the Hindu social system.

It is in the historical and contemporary context of the subordinate position of women in India, and in many other parts of the world, that an examination of the roles and status of Vīraśaiva women would be useful. Most western scholars, including the famous German sociologist Max Weber (1968) and well-known indologists such as R. G. Bhandarkar (1913), have not provided an accurate and fair account of Vīraśaivism and the unique position of Vīraśaiva women. These scholars relied on questionable secondary sources, as they were unable to study, due to lack of knowledge of the Kannada language, the original authentic Vīraśaiva socio-religious and philosophical texts such as the numerous "sayings" or lyrics (*vacanas*) of Vīraśaiva saints and *Śūnyasampādane*. It is only during the past few decades that Vīraśaiva scholarship has been based on primary sources and empirical research. Part III of this book contains a review of studies on Vīraśaivism during the nineteenth and twentieth centuries.

Few major works on the religion or on the women of India provide even a brief sketch of the revolutionary Vīraśaiva movement during the twelfth century. This protest movement, as an object of academic interest, has suffered considerable neglect until recent decades. The Bhakti movement of the twelfth century in Karnatak was spearheaded by its leaders, such as Basava, Mahādevi, Prabhu, Cennabasava, and a host of other Vīraśaiva saints. This social movement emerged as a revolt against all forms of inequality. More than sixty women saint-poets, along with other leaders of this movement, have valiantly advocated and practiced egalitarian ideologies. A galaxy of women mystics have made significant contributions to Vīraśaiva philosophy and society. Vīraśaiva women have not only had equal opportunity, but also followed different paths to spiritual attainment. In the quest for spiritual attainment, women have either adopted the traditional role of housewife or, in some cases, rejected the traditional role. In any case, they have manifested independent spiritual accomplishments. In advocating the liberty and equality of all human beings irrespective of caste, class, and occupation, these social reformers were far ahead of their times. The egalitarian principles of Vīraśaivism have influenced succeeding generations of Vīraśaivas, their community, social system, and culture.

Although there are some valuable studies on the Vīraśaiva religion (Nandimath, 1979), history and philosophy (Sakhare, 1978), literature (Ramanujan, 1973; Zvelebil, 1984), society (Ishwaran, 1983), politics (Parvathamma, 1971), and family and kin network (Chekki, 1974, 1968), to our knowledge there is no sociological study devoted mainly toward an understanding of the status of Vīraśaiva women. *The Bhakti Movement and the Status of Women: A Case Study of Vīraśaivism* (Mullatti, 1989), however, attempts to examine the impact of the Bhakti movement on the roles and status of Vīraśaiva women in a middle sized city in northern Karnatak, India.

Based on a sample of 200 women composed of mothers and daughters, and mothers-in-law and daughters-in-law, a multifaceted profile of Vīraśaiva women is presented. An historical background of the Bhakti movement, and the status of women in the Vīraśaiva community during the twelfth century and the centuries that followed, provides a basis for a better understanding of the status of contemporary Vīraśaiva women. A major portion of this volume examines marriage and family life, and the economic and socio-religious lives of present-day Vīraśaiva women.

The author argues that Vīraśaiva child training, strongly influenced by an egalitarian ideology, contributes to the emergence of an egalitarian "identity" among Vīraśaiva women. Furthermore, an attempt is made to examine how this identity is manifested in different aspects of her life and culture, and the effectiveness of the interactional process of child training on the personality development of Vīraśaiva women.

A Vīraśaiva woman is free to pursue her own religious-spiritual goals. In other words, women have equal rights to attain the ultimate goal of a Vīraśaiva, that is, the complete union of one's self with the Universal Self — Śiva — the only supreme God. Indeed, the Vīraśaiva socialization process and family milieu tend to coalesce in a Vīraśaiva cultural pattern built around the configuration of the relative equality of men and women.

The Vīraśaiva philosophy stresses a close link between the social and spiritual aspects of life. There is no inherent contradiction or conflict insofar as the achievement of family and religious goals are concerned. In this regard, marriage serves as a foundation of the egalitarian Vīraśaiva family. It is noteworthy that husband-wife relations are egalitarian and that the Vīraśaiva family not only accords equal rights to men and women, but also entrusts them with equal responsibilities.

Women's work, both within and outside the family, is guided by the Vīraśaiva work ethic, which stipulates that everyone should work and share the fruits of their labor with family and community. It is observed that the economic conditions of Virasaiva women are not repressive or exploitative, but rather help them to enhance their status in the family and community. In the socio-religious sphere, Vīraśaiva women have equal opportunities, since married life and the work ethic tend to help attain both social and spiritual goals.

More importantly, this study highlights the absence of traditional constraints on Vīraśaiva women that are so characteristic of the Brahmanic Hindu culture. For instance, Vīraśaiva widows do not encounter the social stigma faced by Brahmin widows. Vīraśaiva women do not observe ritual pollution during menstrual periods. Divorce and remarriage are not prohibited. These and other aspects of the Vīraśaiva ideology characterize the distinct status of Vīraśaiva women.

What is the impact of the Vīraśaiva religious ideology on the status of contemporary Vīraśaiva women? This study suggests that the egalitarian ideals of Vīraśaivism have a major influence on child-rearing and personality development. The modern egalitarian ideals of companionship, higher education, and an independent career are accepted by the younger generation of Vīraśaiva girls without major stresses and strains because of the influence of Vīraśaiva ideologies during childhood.

Compared to non-Vīraśaiva women in India, Vīraśaiva women have been more involved in various roles in the family, and economic and socio-religious lives because of the religious ideology and socialization process. Obviously, the processes of modernization, such as the attainment of higher levels of education, employment opportunities, and changes in legislation and public opinion, also have contributed to the narrowing of the gender gap. Despite these relative more egalitarian roles and status of women, especially in the socio-religious sphere, we cannot overlook the inequality of gender that still persists in various other aspects of life. In view of the centuries of domination by the patriarchal system, there is undoubtedly still a long way to go to achieve the goal of gender equality.

This sociological case study is a major effort to arrive at an understanding of the impact of the Vīraśaiva religious ethic on the status and roles of contemporary Vīraśaiva women.It should be noted, however, that the status of contemporary Vīraśaiva women varies from region to region. Education, social class, and life-style seem to have a differential impact on the roles and status of Vīraśaiva women. Further research, using a probability stratified sample and comparative-longitudinal research design, would be necessary to understand the continuing and changing trends in the status of women. Rural and urban, religious, caste and class variables should be considered in any future sociological research. Such a study would not only be able to build on this case study, but could also have far-reaching policy implications.

In the past few decades, Vīraśaiva women have taken advantage of educational opportunities and have achieved considerable upward social mobility. A large majority of them have a university education. The young urban women are twice as likely to have university degrees. The increased educational aspirations, labor force participation, and career orientation of young Vīraśaiva women have altered the traditional gender roles.

Although Vīraśaiva women have not abandoned the family in their quest for careers, there tends to be a conflict between career aspirations and domestic responsibilities with the demands of the labor market. However, women still remain the primary caregivers to their families and carry the major burden of childcare.

Needless to say, among the Vīraśaiva community members in North America, the gender gap is significantly smaller when compared to their counterparts in India. A comparative study of the status and roles of Vīraśaiva women in India and North America would be illuminating. After having examined the traditional and contemporary social structures and cultures of the Vīraśaiva community, let us attempt to project some possible future trends that may influence the shape of the community in the twenty-first century.

15

THE FUTURE OF THE VĪRAŚAIVA COMMUNITY

Continuity and change have been characteristic of the Vīraśaiva community in India. Century after century the community has faced many challenges, and has not only survived but has grown in strength despite the onslaughts of Jainism, Brahmanic Hinduism, Islam, and Christianity. The Vīraśaiva community has withstood the winds of change and remarkably retained its essential cultural ethos.

During the past quarter-century, the Vīraśaiva community has undergone dramatic and cataclysmic changes. Increasing levels of education, occupational mobility, and modern values and attitudes have made a major impact on the religious beliefs and behavior of a large segment of the population. However, religious group identity remains a strong force in the intergroup relationships of Vīraśaivas in India, so the future of millions of Vīraśaivas in India may not be a matter of great concern.

The future of the Vīraśaiva community in North America, however, is of primary concern. Although the Vīraśaiva community in North America is based on a common religion, national origin, history, traditions, symbols, language, and values, it faces an uncertain future mainly because of its small size and intense exposure to North American values and life-styles. The process of assimilation seems to be quite rapid and significant.

In the 1960s, a large majority of Vīraśaivas consciously or unconsciously made an historic decision to migrate to North America. Perhaps most of them did not realize then that their children and succeeding generations of Vīraśaivas would form an integral part of the North American society. Vīraśaivas constitute a small visible minority, that is highly educated and affluent even by North American standards. In the traditional Vīraśaiva family in India, the task of religious training was assumed by parents, the family, and the community. Children were raised in a profoundly religious atmosphere. In North America, however, Vīraśaiva parents do not seem to be adequately prepared for the mammoth task of religious training of the young. The children have already lost their parental language, have changed their dietary habits, and, more importantly, they have very little, if any, knowledge of the Vīraśaiva religion and culture.The younger generation now seems to face an identity crisis. The Vīraśaivas in North America have a greater assimilationist tendency than most other immigrant religious groups. This is likely to lead to eventual cultural suicide, unless they act now. Change is natural and inevitable, but if they disregard the essential edicts of Vīraśaivism, they eventually may be assimilated into the North American culture.

The significance of North American Vīraśaivism must be understood within a wider perspective. For the past three decades, opportunities for the expression and transmission of Vīraśaivism have been very limited. As far as this author knows, most Vīraśaivas of the first generation of immigrants would like to maintain their distinct religion and culture. They reject the goal of assimilation (Gordon, 1964) and attempt to transmit their Vīraśaiva identity onto their children and their children's children.

The efforts of Vīraśaivas to retain an ethnic identity tend to be more strenuous than those of other ethnic groups in North America. However, the North American Vīraśaiva community has a future, provided a concerted effort is made by them. The future of Vīraśaivism in North America depends on the efforts of the present generation, and also on the younger generation of Vīraśaivas who will have their own families in the next century. If they become apathetic and indifferent, assimilation is inevitable. Assimilation may be considered complete when a person no longer considers him/herself as a Vīraśaiva and when others no longer regard him/her as a Vīraśaiva.

The characteristics of the Vīraśaiva community in North America help us to understand the problems it faces, its future, and the prognosis for its survival. From the demographic perspective, Vīraśaivas constitute only a minuscule segment of the North American population. The preeminence of Vīraśaivas rests more upon a cultural symbolic importance than upon any statistical reality or numerical strength. Because of its small size, the problem of community survival cannot be overlooked. Insignificant levels of immigration and a low birth rate imply that Vīraśaivas are most likely to be a small community in the twenty-first century.

The strong geographic concentration of Vīraśaivas in the Northeastern United States somewhat counteracts the problems that stem from their low population size. In other words, this helps to create a network of relationships and services among them, and it may slow the rate of assimilation to a certain extent. However, the India-born generation has to accept the fact that their children are being raised in a North American culture where the school, peer groups, and the mass media, especially TV, are more influential than the family. The educational and occupational achievements have, no doubt, brought great benefits to the Vīraśaiva family and their community, which, in turn, have created several changes in their life-styles. Unfortunately, the new cultural patterns adopted by them have considerably reduced their loyalty and conformity to the Vīraśaiva religion and culture.

Even so, Vīraśaivas have adopted and relinquished cultural patterns selectively. The Vīraśaivas seem to be victims of their own success inasmuch as they feel compelled to surrender the traditional Vīraśaiva cultural patterns as inappropriate or inconvenient to the new environment. In doing so, however, it is essential to see that they are not compromising the fundamental Vīraśaiva principles and practices and their Vīraśaiva identity. This process of adaptation, change, and assimilation (Gordon, 1964) raises special issues for Vīraśaiva identity and survival.

In the Vīraśaiva culture, the obligation of family life is prescribed for everyone. In the absence of indicators to the contrary, it is fair to assume that the Vīraśaiva family is characterized by warmth, respect, and affection between spouses, and between parents and children. The Vīraśaiva values stress cooperation and mutual understanding, and sacrifice for the well-being and solidarity of the family. The number of Vīraśaiva families in North America who read Vīraśaiva texts, practice religious principles, and observe holidays and rituals is unknown. Our guess is that it is very limited. Despite its special character, the Vīraśaiva family is destined to move toward the North American middle-class family model, with its stress on the mutual independence of parents and children and on secular values and behavior. At this point in time, the cohesion and stability of the Vīraśaiva family is remarkable, especially considering the pressure of extraordinary potentials for stress and tension in the mainstream North American society.

A source of strain is the generation gap. While the India-born Vīraśaiva may adapt to the North American culture, the values of the traditional culture are deeply imprinted on one's personality. The child born and/or raised in North America carries no such cultural heritage, and hence the generation gap creates conflicts. However significant all of these changes are for the evolving nature of the Vīraśaiva family, they have their most profound implications in the transmission of the religious identity. Influenced by an "assimilation syndrome," it is doubtful whether the Vīraśaiva family can continue to maintain its function of identity transmission in the next century. It is this shrinking contribution of the Vīraśaiva family to Vīraśaiva identity transmission that constitutes its essential weakness. The feelings of Vīraśaivas about their identity, and their strong desire to see that their children and grandchildren maintain and strengthen the Vīraśaiva identity, could be translated into action so as to create a vibrant Vīraśaiva community in the North American society of the twenty-first century. In view of the imminent Vīraśaiva identity crisis, it is necessary to examine an important question: "What is the future of the Vīraśaiva community in North America?"

If they do not learn from history, they shall be compelled to relive it. But if they do not understand and change the future, they shall be compelled to endure it, and that could be worse. Vīraśaivas can plan for the future provided they draw the future into their consciousness and probe it with all the intelligence and imagination at their command.

The twenty-first century will see the third, fourth, and fifth generations of Vīraśaivas in North America. They will experience a totally different world. A million times more sophisticated thinking computers, robots, artificial intelligence, test-tube babies, surrogate motherhood, genetic engineering, interplanetary communication and travel, interstellar migration, and, perhaps, Star Wars are just a few of the many innovations that are likely to be a reality. The impact of these changes on human relationships, families, and the community is beyond our imagination. The world in the year 2047 will be profoundly different from our own because of tremendous technological advances and social changes.

What is the future of the Vīraśaiva community as it faces the twenty-first century? The social fabric of the Vīraśaiva community will be radically different. We would like to present two models that forecast different possible characteristics of the Vīraśaiva community in the twenty-first century. There could be other possibilities or alternatives.

The Utopian model is based on optimism. This model predicts that almost all Vīraśaivas will maintain a distinct Vīraśaiva identity through knowledge and practice of the Virasaiva religion and culture. This scenario is based on the belief that the present and succeeding generations of Vīraśaivas will make conscious efforts to conform to the essentials of Vīraśaivism, and that they will integrate rather than assimilate. It is projected that the Veerashaiva Samaja of North America will be a strong and well-established organization in the twenty-first century. The Vīraśaiva community may form a cohesive unit like the Jews, Sikhs, Tibetans, Mennonites, and Catholics.

The non-Utopian model is based on a pessimistic belief that most Vīraśaivas will abandon their religion because of apathy, indifference, and gross negligence. The impact of North American mainstream culture, Christianity, intermarriage, and modern secular forces will lead to a loss of Vīraśaiva consciousness and identity. The consequences of the process of assimilation will be cultural suicide. North American Vīraśaivas may become indistinguishable from the mainstream culture as a separate religious and ethnic community. What has happened to African, West Indian, Chinese, and Japanese Americans offer a few examples.

It is more likely that the Vīraśaivas will be heading toward the non-Utopian model unless they make herculean efforts and take seriously the task of educating their young in the Vīraśaiva religion and culture. This is possible if they work toward achieving three major goals: (1) a family deeply embedded in the Vīraśaiva culture, (2) a highly developed organizational structure, and (3) a firmly established Vīraśaiva educational system. These are necessary to nourish a Vīraśaiva consciousness-identity. Vīraśaiva education could be concerned with both formal and informal training in the Vīraśaiva cultural heritage. It is a force that could contribute to the shaping of the Vīraśaiva identity.

Following the Utopian model, a plan for the future could include the following strategies. Study groups could be developed for all age groups to meet regularly for the study of classical Vīraśaiva texts. As an alternative, individuals might continue their Vīraśaiva education by self-study. The Sunday school, youth camps, and, most importantly, religious instruction in the family and community context could play important roles. Vīraśaiva learning for the young could be made more interesting, relevant, creative, innovative, and challenging through the use of printed and audio-video materials, lectures, discussions, computer software, and mass media (TV, radio, press, video, computer Internet) projects. Vīraśaiva learning could be mandatory, and every Vīraśaiva could aim at a basic knowledge of the Vīraśaiva religion, history, and culture.

Many Vīraśaivas are not providing a setting for their children in which the primary learning experience would be of the Vīraśaiva culture. It is necessary to develop an educational system that is both North American and Vīraśaiva. This is, no doubt, a major problem, but not an insurmountable one. For children, the North American culture serves to alienate them from the Vīraśaiva religion and culture.

Parents provide little reinforcement by way of role models. They tend to think of themselves as good Vīraśaivas, but their loyalty to Vīraśaiva tradition tends to be more of a sentimental gesture than a hard commitment. In a long range plan, the scientific and humanistic studies of the Vīraśaiva culture should constitute a major part of the Vīraśaiva educational effort. This is a challenge for all Vīraśaivas in North America.

Courses on the Vīraśaiva religion and culture could be offered at colleges and universities. Chairs of Vīraśaiva studies could be established. Fellowships and awards for Vīraśaiva study and research could be instituted. There is a need for translating religious texts from Kannada into English, especially for the younger generation. The Kannada language could be taught to the young. The Institute for Vīraśaiva Studies, Vīraśaiva journals, encyclopedias, yearbooks, books, periodical publications, libraries, museums, and Virasaiva Foundations are a few among many projects that could be planned and implemented.

The assumption is that an increase in knowledge of the Vīraśaiva religion and culture will bring an increase in commitment to Vīraśaiva values. This plan need not be just an ideal dream. Anyway, it is on dreams that communities and even nations are built. It is a challenge for every Vīraśaiva. These goals can be achieved, provided Vīraśaivas have a strong will and show a selfless dedicated effort. All Vīraśaivas in North America can preserve their culture. Catholics and Jews provide relevant models. They have done admirable work to preserve and enhance their religion and culture.

Vīraśaiva community leaders of the twelfth century had foresight and vision. Their ideas and actions were quite ahead of their time. The ideals espoused and practised by them — such as liberty, equality, the work ethic, community sharing and service, non-violence and peace, rationality, and humanism — are important both today and in the decades and centuries to come. In a society that is becoming increasingly complex, formal, and impersonal, ethnic identification would provide a sense of "gemeinschaft" (Tönnies, 1995) or an affective bond for Vīraśaivas. A majority of North American Vīraśaivas have felt the necessity to preserve and strengthen their cultural heritage. The Vīraśaiva community needs to find a niche in North America and make a significant contribution to the mosaic of North American culture and society. The past flows into the present. The future is open, and the shape of the future Vīraśaiva community will depend on the choices that are made today by a large majority of its members.

The relationship between the intellectual productions and the socio-cultural environment were analyzed by K. Marx, K. Mannheim, M. Scheler, and others. Part III is not intended to be an in-depth exploration into the sociology of knowledge. It provides the contours of some key intellectuals, both "insiders" and "outsiders," and their efforts in developing the knowledge about the Vīraśaiva religious community. Furthermore, it presents a research agenda for the twenty-first century.

Part III

THE COMMUNITY IN
RETROSPECT AND PROSPECT

16

KNOWLEDGE AND SOCIETY

The relationship between human thought and the sociocultural environment within which it arises is a complex one. Knowledge about the Lingāyat religion and culture has been developed, transmitted, and maintained in different social contexts by different people in different time periods. It is necessary to explore and examine the process of knowledge creation and dissemination regarding the Lingāyat religion and society since the early nineteenth century. The presentation that follows is not intended to be a comprehensive survey. It is intended to be representative, rather than exhaustive, in terms of analysis of research trends. The discussion attempts to provide a chronological development of Vīraśaiva studies. It should be regarded as a social map, with only brief outlines of selected contributions to Vīraśaiva studies. This chapter merely scratches the surface of a vital intellectual endeavor.

During the early decades of the nineteenth century, very few people had any idea or knowledge of the vast range and immense magnitude of the Lingāyat or Vīraśaiva literature that had been accumulated over the previous several centuries. Our present knowledge of the Lingāyat religion, literature, and philosophy is the result of meticulous and patient efforts on the part of a small number of committed and painstaking scholars who belonged to the nineteenth and the first half of the twentieth centuries. These scholars, without expectation of material rewards or fame, laboriously brought together the largely inaccessible and scattered information contained in inscriptions on stone and copper and in the texts of numerous palm-leaf manuscripts. Without the pioneering efforts of these scholars, much of this Vīraśaiva treasure would have been lost to posterity.

Despite its long history of consummate literary expression, its fabulous grandeur, and fascinating variety, Lingāyat religion, literature, and society, as an object of systematic study and analysis, is relatively recent in origin. Among the forerunners who studied Lingāyat religion, literature, and society during the nineteenth century were British administrators, German-Swiss Christian missionaries, ethnographers, and scholars interested in Indology.

Colonel Mark Wilks (1980), who served (1750-1831) as an officer of the East India Company in the south of India and also as the British Resident (1803-1808) in the former princely state of Mysore, was probably the first to present a few historical sketches of the Lingāyats under the label "Jangum." He noted that Basava, the founder of this sect, taught a doctrine of monotheism, embodied in the worship of Śiva. The lingam, as the image of Śiva, was always to be borne on the person. His ethical teaching was the abolition of caste. Wilks also observed that the followers of this sect formed a very large proportion of the agricultural and trading populations of Mysore. Furthermore, he stated that the Lingāyats were found scattered in considerable numbers over the Konkan, Kanara, and Deccan, and constituted a considerable portion of the population of Coorg. His knowledge of Lingāyat dynasties was evident when he mentioned the fact that Lingāyatism was a state religion of the Wodeyars of Mysore (1399-1610), of the Nayaks of Keladi and Ikkeri or Bedanur (1550-1763), and the Rajas of Coorg.

Francis Buchanan (1811), another officer of the East India Company who traveled (1807) from Madras through the countries of Mysore, Canara, and Malabar for the express purpose of investigating the state of the religion, manners, and customs along with the history, agriculture, arts and commerce, etc., makes very scanty reference to the Lingāyats. His account is impressionistic, confusing, and misleading.

In the early nineteenth century, Jean Antoine abbe Dubois (1908) spent thirty years (1765-1848) in the various provinces of Southern India. During his long sojourn in India he collected materials and particulars of all sorts pertaining to Hindu manners, customs, and ceremonies. He noted down what he saw, heard, and read, and aimed at simplicity and accuracy. Dubois observed that "the sect of Śiva predominates altogether in several provinces. They abstain from all animal food. Instead of burning their dead, as do most Hindus, they bury them. They do not recognize the laws relating to defilement, which are generally accepted by other castes." He refers to a proverb that says "There is no river for a Lingayat"; meaning that the members of this sect do not recognize, at all events and on many occasions, the virtues and merits of ablutions.

Furthermore, Dubois points out the Lingāyat rejection of the fundamental principle of the Hindu religion, namely the cycle of birth and rebirth or metapsychosis. In consequence, Lingāyats have no anniversary festivals to commemorate the dead. To quote Dubois, "A Lingāyat is no sooner buried than he is forgotten." He also states that the Lingāyat refuse to recognize any caste distinctions, maintaining that the "lingam" makes all men equal. Despite these perceptive observations, Dubois's knowledge about the role of the Guru and Jangamas seems to be based upon cursory and superficial observations.

Another historical sketch of the Lingāyat sect was presented by H. H. Wilson in his essay (1828-1832) on the religious sects of the Hindus published in the *Asiatic Researches* (volumes VI-VII), which was later (1861) reprinted in a monograph entitled *Religious Sects of the Hindus*. Being a mint-master of the East India Company, his account of the sect was based on a "cursory inspection" of a few Lingāyat texts and oral reports. It was obviously sketchy and superficial.

C. P. Brown's detailed "Essay on the Creed, Customs, and Literature of the Jangams," published (1840b) in the *Madras Journal of Literature and Science,* discusses the influence of the fourfold system of caste on the Vīraśaiva religious organization. Brown asserted that the sect, which broke away from the Brahmanical society, was nonetheless influenced by the Brahmanical idea of social distinction based on heredity and privilege. This essay was later used as a source of reference by ethnographers such as R. E. Enthoven and Edgar Thurston.

In the latter half of the nineteenth century, German Christian missionaries, such as Rev. G. Wurth and Rev. F. Kittel, were interested in the Lingāyat literature. It was as early as 1868 that Rev. G. Wurth published an abridged translation of the *Basava Purana* and a somewhat detailed translation of *Cennabasava Purana* in the *Journal of the Royal Asiatic Society* (Bombay Branch). The translation of these two Puranas, though fragmentary and based on unedited manuscripts, promoted further critical study of the sect, its sacred literature, and early history (Nandimath, 1979).

Rev. F. Kittel, who is well known for his monumental *Kannada-English Dictionary*, published (*Indian Antiquary*, 1875a, 1875b) a few Lingāyat legends and an annotated catalogue of a large number of Lingāyat texts that contain a critical examination of the dates of the texts and the type of literary composition of each text.

Barth's book, *Religions of India* (1882), makes a brief reference to the Lingāyat sect. While lamenting on the difficulty of reconstructing the history of the sect on the basis of unhistorical texts and panegyrics, Barth provides a very distorted historical sketch of the sect.

Monier Williams (1883) in his book, *Religious Thought and Life in India*, presents a brief sketch of "Lingavats" (popularly Lingaits), because they wear the Linga in a silver or metallic casket suspended around their necks with a cord, like a necklace. He notes that this sect is opposed to all of the orthodox practices and religious usages of the Hindus, such as caste distinctions, the authority of the Brahmans, the inspiration of the Veda, and the Brahmanical sacrifices, and that they bury instead of burning their dead. In a footnote, he indicates that the "Lingaits" of the present day are said to be returning to caste rules.

Similar brief sketches of the Lingāyats also can be found in R. G. Bhandarkar's *Early History of the Dekkan* (1896). B. L. Rice, Director of Archaeological Researches in Mysore, presents an unauthentic description in the *Mysore and Coorg: A Gazetteer* and in the *Mysore and Coorg from the Inscriptions* (1909). The authors of these brief sketches lacked acquaintance with the basic Vīraśaiva religious literature. For the first time, Dr. J. F. Fleet's (1899) studies of inscriptions in stone provided epigraphic evidence regarding the historicity of Basava and the early religious activities of the Vīraśaiva movement. During the first decade of the twentieth century, H. H. Risley (1908) noted that the Lingāyat sect started developing endogamous castes from about the seventeenth century. L. D. Barnett (1908) stated that the origins of the Vīraśaiva could be attributed to the southward diffusion of the Kashmir school of Śaivism.

R. C. Carr, who was the chief administrator (collector) of the district of Bellary, took great interest in preparing a monograph on Lingāyats that was published in 1906 in Madras. His writings were based primarily on his observations of Lingāyats in the district of Bellary. Edgar Thurston makes extensive use of this monograph in his essay on Lingāyats that forms a part of his (six volumes) *Castes and Tribes of Southern*

India (1909). R. E. Enthoven, Superintendent of the Ethnographic Survey, Bombay, contributed a lengthy article on the "Lingāyats" to the *Encyclopaedia of Religion and Ethics* (1915) and included ethnographic accounts of the Lingāyat religious community in his *The Tribes and Castes of Bombay* (1923).

While Thurston's account primarily refers to Lingāyats in the Bellary district, Enthoven's account is based on his observations of the Lingāyat social organization, customs, and manners in the districts of Dharwar, Belgaum, and Bijapur. Enthoven provides a detailed description of the social structure of the Lingāyats. He points out that the highest social stratum among the Lingāyats is composed of the priests and traders, followed by artisans, peasants, and manual workers.

Several *District Gazetteers* also included a descriptive report on the Lingāyat community. They provided a wealth of information that would serve as historical data for future researchers. These descriptive accounts, although limited in scope, serve as benchmark studies to measure changes in the Lingāyat community.

The *Castes and Tribes of H.E.H. The Nizam's Dominions*, by Syed Siraj Ul, Hassan (1920:383-399), presents an ethnographic survey of the history, internal structure, occupational groups, religion, marriage and divorce, and rites of passage of the Lingāyats. This volume serves as an important source for understanding the regional variations of castes and customs of the Lingāyats as they then prevailed in the districts of Gulbarga, Raichur, and Bidar in the former state of Hyderabad.

It was probably for the first time that R. C. Artal, a member of the Lingāyat community, published a short account of the reformed Śaiva or Vīraśaiva faith in the *Journal of the Anthropological Society of Bombay* (1909). R. G. Bhandarkar's book *Vaishnavism, Śaivism, and Minor Religious Systems* (1913), maintains that the Lingāyat system came into existence before Basava. He speculates that the non-Brahman members of the upper classes, who were opposed to the power wielded by the Brahmans, formed themselves into a new community. Nicol Macnicol's description of the Vīraśaiva, in his volume *Indian Theism* (1915), is very impressionistic and demonstrates his lack of familiarity with the religious sources of Vīraśaivism. Obviously, this has led to many inaccuracies and sweeping generalizations.

The reputed German sociologist Max Weber's early twentieth century study of the religions of India includes several references to the Lingāyat sect. According to Weber (1968:19), "Originally, in the Middle Ages, it represented a type of particularly sharp and principled "protestant" reaction to the Brahmans and the caste order." He points out that Basava, the founder of the Lingāyat sect, denied Vedic ritual and preached the equality of men and women. Furthermore, he observed (1968:304-305) that the Lingāyat doctrine was strictly "monotheistic," recognizing only Śiva and denying the Brahmanical Hinduistic pantheon and the trinity of the highest gods. Weber also emphasized the preeminent role of the Guru among the Lingāyats. With his characteristic breadth of vision, Weber notes that the Lingāyat sect was once again pressed back into the caste order by the power of the environment.

Weber presents a process of the reemergence of a caste order among the Lingāyats. First, there developed an aristocracy of the sibs of the ancient believer over and against the newer converts. Second, status differentiation according to profession occurred. Third, the sect was organized simply according to the traditional castes. He concludes that the rationalistic course, which expressed itself in the provision of the sect, was not able to shatter the massive hagiolatry and traditionalism of its predominantly peasant adherence. Weber admits that the special literature of the sect was, unfortunately, unavailable to him.

E. P. Rice, in his book *A History of Kannada Literature* (1921), devotes two chapters to Lingāyat religion and literature. For him, Basava, the reputed founder of the Lingāyat faith, is in reality only one of its revivers. He provides an overview of the fundamental doctrines and practices of the Vīraśaiva religion, some specimens of the *vacana* literature, and the contributions of Lingāyat writers (1160-1600) to the Kannada literature.

J. N. Farquhar, in his earlier volume (1915:301) on *Modern Religious Movements in India*, indicates that "Basava founded a new sect called the Vīraśaivas and that the members renounced caste altogether; but that the old poison has crept in amongst them again." He emphasizes the role played by the Lingāyat education associations and hostels in Dharwar, Bombay, Mysore, and Bangalore for the promotion of modern education within the community. He also notes the All-India Veerashaiva Conference and its discussions of religious, educational, economic, and other secular problems that affect the life and standing of the sect.

Sir James Campbell (1918) wrote in *Times of India* about Basava's religious and social reform movement. According to him, "neither social conferences held today in several parts of India nor Indian social reformers can improve upon the programme that Basava sketched and boldly tried to work out in a large and comprehensive programme of social reform." For Campbell, "the present day social reformer in India is but speaking the language and seeking to enforce the mind of Basava."

J. N. Farquhar's (1925) *An Outline of the Religious Literature of India* stresses the status of the Jangamas and their monopoly over all sacerdotal functions and privileges among the Lingāyats. He also draws attention to the influence of Jainism on the Vīraśaivas. S. K. Ayyangar (1923) makes reference to the influence of the northern school of Śaivism, especially that of Bengal Śaivism on Vīraśaivism.

Most of these Western writers on the Lingāyat religion and culture, with the exception of a few, provided meager ethnographic accounts. Most of these observations were superficial, ethnocentric, distorted, and misleading. Since they had inadequate knowledge of Kannada and Sanskrit, they did not have access to the original sources of the Vīraśaiva religion and philosophy, and hence were unable to develop a holistic perspective of the religious doctrines and practice. Little effort was made to study the subject with historical or social-scientific objectivity and critical comprehension.

A few indigenous scholars, in the absence of authentic translations of the Vīraśaiva texts, in English presented brief, sometimes panegyric, sketches of the Lingāyat religion. *Indian Philosophy* (1927:730) by Professor S. Radhakrishnan, makes a brief reference to "the reform movement of Basava (in the twelfth century) which was marked by its revolt against the supremacy of the Brahmin." He notes that this sect does not accept the hypothesis of rebirth. As a footnote, he adds, "Though the Lingāyat reformation started with a vigorous protest against the caste system, the Lingāyats today observe caste distinctions."

V. C. Yagati (1928) published an article on "Basava: The Reviver of Lingāyatism" in *The Indian Social Reformer*. He argued that Basava was preeminently a social reformer. Basava, according to him, was a rare combination of a religious reformer, political genuis, great philosopher, and social reformer.

It was in the late 1920s that S. C. Nandimath submitted his thesis on Vīraśaivism and obtained a doctorate degree from the University of London. S. D. Pawate published a book focusing on *Vīraśaiva Philosophy of the Śivagamas*. During the 1930s, although there were many publications in Kannada, works on Vīraśaivism in English seem to have been at their lowest ebb. Among a very few, we may refer to R. Chakravarti's *Śaktivisistādwaita or the Philosophical Aspect of Vīraśaivism* and Hardekar Manjappa's edited collection of articles entitled *Social Structure of the Vīraśaiva Saints*. During this period, selected *vacanas* of Basava were translated into English by T. H. M. Sadashivayya and M. V. Iyengar, but they remained inaccessible to the majority of readers.

The volumes entitled *The Mysore Tribes and Castes*, prepared by L. K. Anantha Krishna Iyer and H. V. Nanjundayya (1931), provide a lengthy chapter on the Lingāyats covering the origin and history of the community, population size and distribution, internal structure of the community, marriage customs and ceremonies, family life, Vīraśaiva tenets, Lingāyat monasteries (*Mathas*), and occupation and social status. It also includes interesting ethnographic accounts and photographs relating to the appearance, dress, and ornaments of the Lingāyats of the princely state of Mysore.

Lewis O'Malley, in his book *Popular Hinduism* (1935), while discussing sectarianism and toleration, observed that the Lingāyats are a distinctive sect. Its adherents may be described justly as Protestants, for not only did they protest originally against caste distinctions, but they also protested against the Brahmans. He notes that within the course of centuries, caste differentiation has been revived, and that the Lingāyats employ their own priests and have ceremonies for births and deaths that are different from those of orthodox Hinduism.

The decade of the 1940s witnessed an outburst of intellectual activity in terms of the publication of books and articles on Vīraśaivism in English. The impetus for such an upsurge originated with the formation of the Literary Committee of the Lingāyat Education Association at Dharwar. The Committee undertook the editing and publication of Vīraśaiva classic works, and the publication of books such as S. C. Nandimath's *A Handbook of Vīraśavism* and M. R. Sakhare's *History and Philosophy of Lingāyat Religion*.

Professor S. S. Basavanal edited the *Journal of the Literary Committee,* which contained articles in both English and Kannada. This quarterly journal, for almost a decade (1941-1948), served as a publication outlet for disseminating studies on Vīraśaivism, not only for the Kannada-speaking region but also for the English-speaking world. V. B. Halabhavi, S. D. Pawate, V. C. Yagati, K. Veerabhadrappa, Kumaraswamiji, A. N. Krishna Rao, and many others frequently contributed to this journal. The journal also published, probably for the first time, the rendering of the Vīraśaiva magnum opus *"Shoonyasampādane,"* in English, by V . C. Yagati. By the end of the 1940s this journal, unfortunately, ceased publication. During the same period, Kumaraswamiji published a series of books on Vīraśaiva philosophy and mysticism.

S. C. Nandimath's *A Handbook of Vīraśavism* is considered to be the first authoritative exposition of the Lingāyat religion, based on an exhaustive study of the original Kannada and Sanskrit sources. The author examines the early history, rituals, and philosophy of the sect. He develops the thesis of pre-Basavan and post-Basavan Vīraśaivism, and of the revival of the former by Basava in the twelfth century. This book has become a frequent source of reference on the subject.

Professor M. R. Sakhare's *History and Philosophy of Lingāyat Religion* traces the history of Śaivism in all of its various phases, and deals with the Lingāyat reform of Śaivism "with great sympathy and keen insight." Professor Sakhare maintains that the Lingāyat religion, although an offshoot of Śaivism, is distinct; and that it should not be considered to be a part of Hinduism insofar as it rejects the Vedas and the distinctions of caste, image worship, and polytheism. He shows that Lingāyatism is not merely a sect, but an integrated system by itself.

Unlike Dr. Nandimath, Professor Sakhare's main thesis is that Basava was the founder of the religion in view of the prophetic turn he gave to Vīraśaivism, the new interpretation of Śatsthala, and the social revolution he brought about. Sakhare was motivated to write and publish his book because the Lingāyat religion was not well known outside Karnatak. He felt that even Lingāyats do not know much about their religious history and philosophy.

In addition to these major works on the Lingāyat religion and philosophy, during the decade of the 1940s, Professor S. S. Basavanal and K. R. Srinivas Iyengar published a translation of the selected *vacanas* of Basava, and S. M. Hunshal published a volume on the Lingāyat movement.

During the 1950s, a few books on India's religions, history, philosophy, and mysticism included brief sketches on Vīraśaivism. A. P. Karmarkar's *The Religions of India* drew a distinction between the mystic and philosophical thoughts of the sect and indicated that the school of mysticism was promulgated by the first five prophets of the sect; and that it was Basava who built a philosophical edifice over this school.

A. L. Basham (1954), in his book *The Wonder That Was India*, mentions some of the striking features of the Lingāyats. He notes that Basava opposed image worship, and rejected the Vedas and the authority of the Brahmins. He opposed pilgrimage and sacrifice, instituted complete equality among his followers, and permitted remarriage of widows. With reference to the practice of burial of the dead among the Lingāyats, Basham speculates, without providing any evidence, that it is possible that Basava was influenced by what he had heard of Islam. Furthermore, Basham observes that the Lingāyats still retain their individuality, although they now have compromised with orthodoxy in some respects.

Surendranath Dasgupta's scholarly account of, *A History of Indian Philosophy* (Volume V) (1955), provides an analysis of the history and literature of Vīraśaivism based on sources in the Sanskrit language only. According to him, the kernel of Vīraśaiva thought was almost as early as the Upanishads. Dasgupta observed that Vīraśaivism differs from the Agamic Śaivism and the Pashupata system in its philosophy and its doctrine of *"sthala,"* the special kind of *"Lingadhārana,"* and also in some other ritualistic matters. Although he has made a good effort in presenting a fairly succinct summary of the history and philosophy of Vīraśaivism, his analysis suffers from several inaccuracies and errors about the Vīraśaiva religion because of his inability to read the Vīraśaiva texts in the Kannada language.

K. A. N. Shastri, in his *A History of South India*, rejects the belief that the sect was founded in hoary antiquity by the five apostles. M. V. Krishnarao, in his *The Mystic Tradition*, refers to the Ārādhya members of the Vīraśaivas as a conservative group with greater reliance on the Vedic authority, and notes the conflict of interest between the orthodox and unorthodox Lingāyats.

The school of thought which claims that the origins of Vīraśaivism lie in the distant past, prior to the twelfth century, tends to rely more on Sanskrit sources such as Upanishads, Śivāgamas, Siddhānta Sikhāmani, Śrikara Bhāsya, and so on. The school of thought that believes Basava to be the founder of the Vīraśaiva religion tends to recognize the Kannada sources, such as the numerous *vacanas* of Vīraśaiva saints, *Śūnyasampādane*, and other religious and philosphical works on Vīraśaivism that have emerged since the twelfth century.

During the 1950s, Kumaraswamiji continued to write on the Vīraśaiva religion and philosophy. Biographies of Basava by V. B. Halabhavi and Chennamallikarjun, Jayaram, and S. S. Malwad were published. C. D. Uttangi's writings on the religious and social significance of *Anubhava Mantapa* made an impact. C. S. Bagi translated a few *vacanas* of Basava. By the early 1950s, V. C. Yagati completed the task of translating into English more than 900 *vacanas* of Basava. This work still remains in typescript. In this decade, two theses on Vīraśaivism were submitted for a doctorate degree by K. Chandrasekhariah and S. M. Hunshal. While the latter was published, the former remains unpublished.

It seems that there were no journals in English that were devoted primarily to the study of the Vīraśaiva religion and society during the 1950s and 1960s. William McCormack's interesting study (in the 1950s) on the forms of communication in the Vīraśaiva religion was published in the United States. His essay, "Lingāyats as a Sect" appeared in the *Journal of the Royal Anthropological Institute* in the early 1960s. We also have come across the *Quarterly Journal of the All India Vīraśaiva Conference*, which hardly published articles in English. It appears to have ceased publication within a few years of its inception.

In the early twentieth century, it was R. Narasimhacharya, Director of Archeological Researches in Mysore, who published a multivolume history of the Kannada poets. Derived primarily from palm-leaf manuscripts, he provided some glimpses of the rich literary heritage in Kannada. Among these literary treasures were numerous works on Vīraśaivism, in general, and the *vacana* literature, in particular, which awaited further exploration, careful scrutiny, and systematic analysis by future generations of scholars.

This survey would be incomplete if we did not discuss even briefly the efflorescence of studies of Vīraśaiva classics by a group of indigenous scholars. This phase of Vīraśaiva studies, extending from the 1920s to the early 1950s, was crucial for laying a solid foundation for further research. The indigenous scholars who were interested in Vīraśaiva studies formed a social network or, rather, what may be called an "invisible college." They came together on the basis of their interests, rather than propinquity or occupational status. The exact boundaries of this scholarly community are difficult to delineate. There was no formal leadership, although there were some central figures.

Some of these pioneers were the first generation of graduates exposed to Western education. They were also educated in Sanskrit and Kannada literature. These intellectuals led a modest life, devoting most of it to the study of the Vīraśaiva religion and culture. They attempted to provide new and comparative perspectives on the Vīraśaiva religion by adopting approaches and frameworks that were characteristic of Western thought and logic. They had neither royal patronage nor huge research grants. They were without institutional support and were devoid of modern library facilities. They did not aspire to academic recognition, fame or fortune. Publication facilities for them were extremely limited. But they were deeply interested in the study of Vīraśaiva literature, and passionately believed that the tenets of the Vīraśaiva religion are of a universal value that needs to be disseminated.

It is necessary to present a brief outline of the significant contributions made by some of the outstanding scholars who belonged to the first generation of indigenous researchers. One group of researchers was composed of scholars such as P. G. Halakatti, S. D. Pawate, V. Bileangadi, V. C. Yagati, V. B. Halabhavi, S. C. Nandimath, M. R. Sakhare, S. S. Basavanal, Kumaraswamiji, R. R. Diwakar, M. R. Shrinivas Murthy, and others. Another group included learned persons such as P.R. Karibasava Shastri, Chennamallikarjuna, B. Shivamurthy Shastri, Buddhayya Puranik, Hardekar Manjappa, Uttangi Chennappa, and others.

Among these indigenous scholars, P. G. Halakatti is aptly recognized as the founding father of the study of *vacana* literature. Up until the early decades of the twentieth century, the Vīraśaiva literature, in palm-leaf manuscript form, was concealed in numerous Lingāyat monasteries and households. The average Lingāyats and even the minuscule scholarly community were unaware of this rich literary legacy pertaining to the Vīraśaiva religion.

It was P. G. Halakatti who painstakingly recovered numerous manuscripts and carefully researched, edited, and published more than 165 books, amounting to about 2500 printed pages. Halakatti collected more than 1000 palm-leaf manuscripts. After almost two decades of research, he published in four volumes the quintessence of *vacana* literature. He abandoned his legal practice, sold his house to pay for a printing press, and in 1926 he started *Śivānubhava*, a journal devoted to Vīraśaiva studies. This journal provided a formal communication outlet, attracted interested scholars, and oriented their intellectual activities toward the study of Vīraśaivism.

For almost three decades this periodical published numerous articles and books on the Vīraśaiva religion and culture. P. G. Halakatti's extensive researches and commentaries on Vīraśaiva saints and *vacanas* are of great historical value to the present generation of scholars. More than twenty-five volumes of *Śivānubhava* alone could be used as the Vīraśaiva Encyclopaedia. Even in the best of times, this journal was subscribed to by no more than 300 institutions and individuals. Despite acute financial problems, he continued to work selflessly as a researcher, editor, and publisher. Through his remarkable contribution to Vīraśaiva studies, he became an institution, a legendary figure. In the 1950s, the Karnatak University, in recognition of his lifetime work, conferred upon him the degree of doctor of philosophy honoris causa, which he richly deserved.

Professor S. S. Basavanal, who was one of the founders of the Karnatak Lingāyat Education Society, continued the tradition of Vīraśaiva research. As a professor of history and a colleague of M. R. Sakhare and S. C. Nandimath, he researched and edited several Vīraśaiva classics, including a revised edition of the *Vacanas* of Basava and a translation into English of selected *Vacanas* of Basava. More importantly, he edited the *Journal of the Literary Committee*, which included many important articles on Vīraśaivism. In the 1940s, this Anglo-Vernacular quarterly journal played an important role in stimulating interest in Vīraśaiva studies.

During a period of a quarter-century (1925-1950), some of the seminal works on Vīraśaivism that made a major impact on the intellectual community and the intelligent reading public were P. G. Halakatti's *Quintessence of Vacana Literature* (Vacana śāstra sāra), R. R. Diwakar's *Secrets of Vacana Literature* (Vacana śāstra Rahasya), and M. R. Srinivās Mūrti's *The Essence of Vacana Literature* (Vacana dharma sāra). These books have become sources of frequent reference in the field of Vīraśaiva studies.

Another tradition of Vīraśaiva studies can be identified in the contributions made by persons such as P. R. Karibasava Shastri. Well versed in Sanskrit and Kannada, he wrote or edited, with explanatory notes and commentaries, more than fifty books related to Virasaivism. He established the Shankar Vilas Press and published a monthly journal called *Vīraśaiva Mata Prakashika*. Through his articles on contemporary issues facing the community, published in this and other journals, he stimulated the Vīraśaiva consciousness.

Hardekar Manjappa read the works of J. S. Mill, Herbert Spencer, and Max Mueller, along with those works by Vīraśaiva saints and Mahatma Gandhi. He authored or edited more than fifty books, many of which were on Vīraśaivism. He is credited to be the first to publish (1924) a biography of Basava. He brought out a beautifully printed miniature booklet containing selected Basava *Vacanas*. More than 100,000 copies of this booklet were distributed free of charge! He helped popularize the celebration of the birthday of Basava and advocated for the eradication of caste distinctions. His many books on the Vīraśaiva religion and society appealed to both children and adults.

Chenna Mallikarjuna is another notable scholar who dedicated his life to the publication and dissemination of Vīraśaiva literature. He edited a journal entitled *Saddharma Deepike* for thirty years. He edited and published more than eighty classical and medieval Vīraśaiva works in his journal. His own works shed new light on the life and times of Basava, Revanasiddha, and Mayideva.

Buddhayya Puranik is known for his works on the life and times of Allama Prabhu. He is the author or editor of as many as twelve volumes on Allama Prabhu. He also published a series of articles, mainly comparative and critical studies of the Vīraśaiva and Maharashtra saints. Uttangi Chennappa, a Christian missionary, made a major contribution by researching and editing the *Vacanas* of Sarvajna, as well as the works of Siddharāma, Molige Mārayya, and others. He provided a comparative analysis of the Lingāyat and Christian religions, and showed the important role of Basava in the emancipation of the untouchables. Moreover, his publication on the historicity and religious significance of Anubhava Mantapa is considered to be a significant contribution.

B. Shivamurthy Shastri, another Kannada-Sanskrit scholar, started a periodical called *Śarana Sāhitya*, devoted to Vīraśaiva studies. For more than a quarter-century he also wrote and edited several books on Vīraśaivism. This journal played an important role in publishing the history, biography, religion, philosophy, and culture of Vīraśaivas in Southern Karnatak.

This brief outline of the indigenous research traditions, characteristic of the period between 1920 and 1955, indicates two streams that seem to interact and overlap in many respects. Since the mid-1950s, much of the Vīraśaiva research seems to emanate largely from universities, and in a very limited way, from monastic organizations and individual researchers. It is beyond the scope of this chapter to examine the collosal literary output on Vīraśaivism in Kannada during the past forty-five years.

17

INTELLECTUALS AND CULTURE

Intellectuals, according to Edward Shils, are indispensible to any society. Intelligentsia include "all those who create, describe and apply culture, the creator of the culture, such as the scholars and authors" (Lipset, 1959:460). As gatekeepers of ideas, the creative intelligentsia are concerned with the values of the society enshrined in its culture. For our purpose, we shall simply define intellectuals as those with a special interest in a systematic study of the Vīraśaiva religion and culture, and those involved in teaching and doing research in the humanities and social sciences. Intellectuals have played a pivotal role in the creation, diffusion, and utilization of knowledge on the Vīraśaiva religion and culture. The following is intended to provide an overview of the patterns of research on the Lingāyat society and culture since the 1960s. A full-scale review of the works cited here is beyond the scope of this study.

The decade of the 1960s inaugurated a new phase of Vīraśaiva studies, and the Karnatak University served as a nucleus for scholars interested in these studies. By now, the era of the lone researcher without institutional aid seemed to be on the wane. A new generation of academics entrusted with the task of teaching, as well as research, came into existence. At the university level, team research, endowed with library facilities, research grants, and research assistants, was made possible. This institutional affiliation and support for research also procured financial resources for publication activities. Prior to the 1950s, the lone Vīraśaiva scholars had none of these institutional supports for their research and publication endeavors.

Under the leadership of Dr. D. C. Pawate, Vice-Chancellor of Karnatak University, and with substantial research grants from the University Grants Commission, it was possible to undertake a large-scale project of editing and publishing the numerous *vacanas* of Vīraśaiva saints and some important Vīraśaiva literary classics. With munificent donations from the community, the university was able to establish a chair in Vīraśaivism, as well as the Basaveshwara chair. Professors R. C. Hiremath, M. S. Sunkapur, and a few others were responsible for editing a series of Vīraśaiva literary classics.

Almost simultaneously, another project of great magnitude was undertaken by the Karnatak University in the 1960s. The University Grants Commission also provided funds for the translation of *Śūnyasampādane* into English. Professors S. C. Nadimath, R. C. Hiremath, Armando Menezes, M. S. Sunkapur, and S. S. Bhoosnurmath, coupled with a team of assistants, accomplished the task of translating this Vīraśaiva magnum opus into English. During this decade selected *vacanas* of Basava were translated into English by A. S. Theodore and D. Hakari, Armando Menezes, and S. M. Angadi. In 1967, both Menezes and Angadi published a translation of all of the *vacanas* of Basava. Allama Prabhu's selected *vacanas* were translated into English by L. Basavaraju.

Romila Thapar's *History of India* made reference to the formation of the Vīraśaiva sect as a positive consequence to the evolution of social institutions in the Middle Ages. She observed that the liberal social outlook of the Vīraśaiva sect won the support of many lower classes of people. P. B. Desai (1968), another historian, in his book *Basaveshwara and His Times* presented important inscriptional and literary evidence related to the early life of Basava.

Thus far, it is evident that an overwhelming majority of the students of Vīraśaiva studies focused on the religious history, philosophy, and literature, and on the life of Basava. The decade of the 1960s is significant because, for the first time, sociological empirical researches on the contemporary Lingāyat community and culture were undertaken. Professor K. Ishwaran (1966, 1968) embarked upon an ambitious program of research. As part of an integrated plan based upon rich sources of field material and comparative cross-cultural studies of economic systems, he presented a clear account of peasant tradition and economy, in general, and the social structure and dynamics of Lingāyats, in particular. As part of a research project on the impact of modernization, Chekki (1968, 1969) made a comparative analysis of the Lingāyat (and Brahmin) family and kinship systems and published several articles on Lingāyat marriage, family, and the impact of legislation in various professional journals in India and abroad. H. M. Sadasivayya (1967) published a sociological study of two Vīraśaiva monasteries.

In the decade of the 1970s, we witnessed an upsurge of research and publication in the field of Vīraśaiva studies insofar as books, periodical literature, and theses are concerned. First, it is noteworthy that books on the biography and contribution of Basava by M. Chidanand Murthy, S. S. Wodeyar, S. S. Malwad, and H. Thipperudraswamy, and the biography and philosophical contributions of Cennabasava by R. C. Hiremath, were published. Furthermore, the biographies of Yedeyur Siddalingaswami, Hangal Kumar Swami, and Dharwad Mrutyunjaya Swami also appeared. Almost all of these works are highly readable and authentic accounts of these central figures, both medieval and modern. The Government of Mysore, under the leadership of B. D. Jatti and S. Nijalingappa, who served as chief ministers of the Mysore State (Wodeyar, 1967), published a volume on the life and philosophy of Basava while commemorating the eighth centenary of Sri Basaveshwara. It provides a unique comparative perspective on the world's religious leaders and philosophers. During this decade two theses were submitted, one on the grammar of *vacana* literature and another on Śivayoga as espoused and practiced by Vīraśaiva mystics.

Next, we come across a series of translations of selected *vacanas* of Akka Mahadevi, Siddalingeshwara, and Siddarāma by Professor Armando Menezes, who for a long time served as a Professor of English at Karnatak College and later at Karnatak University. These translations into English were done in close collaboration with S. M. Angadi. During the same period, Professor A. K. Ramanujan translated selected *vacanas* of Basavanna, Devara Dāsimayya, Mahādeviyakka, and Allama Prabhu. These translations were published with an introduction and an essay on "On Lingāyat Culture" by William McCormack, under the title *Speaking of Śiva*. As this volume was published in the Penguin Classics series, it received wider attention in the scholarly community, especially in North America and Europe.

In the early 1970s, the final volume of *Śūnyasampādane* appeared. Based on Śiva Agamas, the volume, entitled *Essentials of Vīraśaivism*, was published by H. P. Malledevaru. It contains a discussion of the fundamental doctrines of the Vīraśaiva philosophy and religion. S. C. Nandimath's *A Handbook of Vīraśaivism* was reprinted (1979) along with a new introduction by R. N. Nandi.

A publication entitled *Kapalikas and Kalamukhas*, relevant to Vīraśaivism, appeared in the early 1970s. Based on epigraphic and historical sources, David N. Lorenzen presented a detailed account of these two lost Śaivite sects that had probably prevailed until the thirteenth century. According to him, a considerable amount of circumstantial evidence points to the existence of a close historical link between the Kalamukhas and the Vīraśaivas. Lorenzen identified important similarities between the Kalamukhas and Vīraśaivas, such as the organization into large monasteries (*mathas*), the emphasis placed on Linga worship, and the priests called Jangamas, with the same interpretation. Furthermore, he observed that many former Kalamukha temples are now controlled by the Vīraśaivas.

Among the sociological works, a volume on the populistic community and modernization by K. Ishwaran (1977) completed the author's trilogy and revealed some of the core values and changing behavior of Lingāyats. D. A. Chekki's volume on modernization and kin network (1974) demonstrated how the process of modernization among Lingāyats revealed the fusion of traditional and modern values and behavior. Parvathamma (1971, 1972, 1978) published a couple of works on the Lingāyat social structure, religion, and politics. Venugopal (1977) published an essay on the factor of anti-pollution in the ideology of the Lingāyat movement.

There was also increased sociological research productivity in terms of doctoral theses. For instance, Arun Bali examined the Vīraśaiva movement in the sect-church framework, and showed how the movement brought about changes in religion, social ethics, education, economy, and polity. G. S. Bidarakoppa, G. Shivarudrappa, and Sadyojata swami focused on the role of the Vīraśaiva monasteries (*mathas*) and their contribution to religion, education, and social welfare. V. S. Kambi wrote on Virasaiva philosophy. K. Lalithamba and Rathnasabhapathy explored Vīraśaivism in Andhra and Tamil Nadu, respectively. While Margaret T. Egmor wrote a thesis on the acquisition of power and prestige by the Lingāyats. R. Blake Michael prepared a thesis on the pattern of religious association in fifteenth-century Vīraśaivism. Both of these theses were submitted to Harvard University.

With the closing of the publication of the *Journal of the Literary Committee* in the late 1940s, for almost a quarter-century there was no major periodical in the English language primarily devoted to Vīraśaiva studies. Basava Samiti, a premier organization designed to disseminate the universal principles of Basava, was established in the mid-1960s. Under the leadership of Dr. B. D. Jatti, former Vice President of India, this organization has grown in size and in terms of its contribution toward the publication and distribution of Vīraśaiva literature. It started the much needed *Basava Journal* in 1976. This journal has stimulated much interest in Vīraśaiva studies. As the only leading journal in the field, it has published numerous articles on a wide variety of issues related to Basava and Vīraśaivism. A large majority of articles are still on Basava and his reform movement, and were written by M. Chidanand Murthy, B. D. Jatti, Siddayya Puranik, V. K. Gokak, S. S. Wodeyar, R. T. Jangam, and others. T. V. Mallappa published papers on the Virasaiva religion and philosophy, while Sarojini Shintri and Leela Mullatti wrote on Vīraśaiva women. Of the Western scholars and their contribution to this journal, mention can be made of William Martha's comparative analysis of Vīraśaivism and Christianity, M. P. Samartha's study on Basava and the process of final liberation in Vīraśaivism, and R. Blake Michael's essays on Vīraśaiva traditions. All in all, under the editorshp of Dr. Siddayya Puranik, a poet-scholar and a former senior member of the government's administrative service, the *Basava Journal* was able to attract a considerable number of contributors and readers during the 1970s and 1980s.

The decade of the 1980s appeared to see a shift in emphasis and focus with regard to studies on the Vīraśaiva religion, literature, and society. An interesting new trend is the publication of translations into English of a series of novels about Vīraśaiva saints. A prolific writer, Professor H. Thipperudraswamy, who has contributed several scholarly works on Vīraśaivism, happens to be the author of these novels on the life of major Vīraśaiva saints. C. N. Hiremath has translated most of these novels into English.

Likewise, G. B. Sajjan provided a translation of a monograph on Mahādevi by Dr. S. Puranik. Sarajoni Shintri's work on Akka Mahādevi, and Prabhu Prasad's publication on Sarvajna, also need to be considered as distinct contributions to Vīraśaiva studies. Leela Mullatti's volume, entitled *The Bhakti Movement and the Status of Women*, is another useful sociological case study of contemporary Vīraśaiva women's status and roles.

Another notable contribution is Dr. K. V. Zvelebil's translation of selected *vacanas* of Basavanna, entitled *The Lord of the Meeting Rivers*. This work was sponsored by the United Nations' Educational Scientific and Cultural Organization (UNESCO). The translator, an internationally known scholar of Dravidian linguistics, has tried to keep faith with the original in structure, form, and content. He also provides a clear and succinct outline of the Vīraśaiva philosophy and doctrine. This translation contains a representative sample of Basava's social thought and the depth of his mystic experience.

The Basaveshwara Chair established at Karnatak University under the direction of Professor M. M. Kalburgi has provided a forum for on-going research and publication of a series of works on Vīraśaivism in English, French, Spanish, and other

Indian and foreign languages. The Institute of Vīraśaiva Studies, which forms a part of Sri Jagad Guru Tontadarya Matha, Gadag, also has published numerous books on the Vīraśaiva religion, biographies of community leaders, and Vīraśaiva literature.

More importantly, Ishwaran's volume, *Religion and Society Among the Lingāyats of South India* (1983), should be recognized as a major contribution to the history and sociology of religion. This work admirably portrays the uniqueness of the Lingāyat religion. The author advances the thesis that the Lingāyat tradition is a blend of the Great and Little traditions, and as a populistic religion is characterized by an absence of hierarchy, and also that the Lingāyat community is well integrated into the social fabric of the larger society.

In the 1980s, the *Basava Journal* continued to publish a series of articles by S. Puranik, S. S. Wodeyar, C. N. Hiremath, Bill Aitkin, Robert Martin, M. P. Samartha, G. B. Sajjan, Sarojini Shintri, Thipperudraswamy, and others. Articles on Basava still predominate. However, an increasing number of articles on Allama Prabhu, Akkamahādevi, Nijaguna Sivayogi, and other male and female saints, and comparative studies of Basava in relation to Buddha, Karl Marx, and Gandhi, as well as Vīraśaiva cosmology, and so on, also are being published. It appears that B. Virupakshappa, the current chief editor of the *Basava Journal*, has been attempting to expand it's scope and distribution. He has made an appeal to the students of Vīraśaiva studies to contribute more original essays, along with a request to the public to subscribe to the journal in greater numbers.

Of the periodical literature on the Lingāyat ideology and society that appeared in the 1980s, Venugopal's study of the Lingāyat ideology of salvation and of the monastic organization, and the longitudinal researches of D. A. Chekki on change and continuity of the Lingāyat family both in India and in North America, deserve mention. After more than seventy years of Enthoven's article on the Lingāyats, published (1915) in the *Encyclopaedia of Religion and Ethics*, a new set of reference volumes, entitled the *Encyclopaedia of Religion* (1987), included an article on "Vīraśaivas" by Andre Padoux. Unlike Enthoven's lengthy exposition, this article is brief and sketchy and forms part of a general discussion on the various branches of Śaivism.

S. R. Gunjal's *Lingāyat Bibliography: A Comprehensive Sourcebook* (1989) provides an impressive compilation of all books and articles on the Lingāyat religion and culture published in English, German, French, Telugu, Tamil, Sanskrit, Marathi, Hindi, and Urdu. This reference volume is useful in identifying gaps in research and for establishing priorities for Vīraśaiva studies in the next several decades.

During the 1960s, a substantial number of Vīraśaivas migrated to the United States and Canada for advanced education and work. As stated previously, in the late 1970s a group of concerned American Vīraśaivas established an association called the Veerashaiva Samaja of North America (VSNA), with the avowed purpose of preserving and propagating the religious, social, educational, and cultural activities, and fostering multicultural understanding, appreciation, and cultural exchange between the people of North America and India, in particular the Vīraśaivas. This organization has been publishing a periodical entitled *Veerashaiva*. It is an important communication medium that contains articles on the history and philosophy of Vīraśaivism, Basava, and other Vīraśaiva male and female saints, and change and continuity among the Lingāyat families and youth in North America. The souvenirs of annual conference proceedings and membership directories also have enabled Vīraśaivas to develop social networks and kinship bonds. In recent years, it also has published a few books on the Vīraśaiva religion and philosophy. During the 1980s, it seems that, for the first time outside India, an organized effort was made to facilitate the publication of studies related to the Vīraśaiva religion and culture. In the 1990s, the Veerashaiva Samaja of North America has continued the task of disseminating Vīraśaiva culture by publishing a periodical and some monographs of interest to its members.

As we enter the last decade of the twentieth century a new semi-annual journal, called *Sarana*, has made its debut. This journal, under the chief editorship of Dr. H. Thipperudraswamy, hopes to present a comprehensive account of the Vīras'aiva religion, literature, philosophy, society, and culture to the English-speaking world. The first issue (June 1990) contains articles on Vīraśaivism, Vīraśaiva saints, and places of historical interest for Vīraśaivas. The journal is published by the Jagadguru Sri Shivaratreshwara Mahavidya Peetha, Mysore, and has been retitled *Sarana Patha*.

Śiva's Warriors (1990) by V. Narayana Rao and Gene Roghair provides readable translations from the *Basava Purana* in the Telugu language. It includes a hagiographical legendary biography of Basava, along with many other stories of Śaiva devotees. *Revolution of the Mystics* (1991), by Jan Peter Schouten, investigates aspects of the Vīraśaiva views on caste, the interpretation of work and service, the position of women, and the educational ideals as advocated by the Vīraśaiva saints and poets of the twelfth and fifteenth centuries. He also examines the influence of the Vīraśaiva norms on the community during the nineteenth and twentieth centuries.

*The Origins of Vīraśaiva Sect*s (1992) by R. Blake Michael is another study focusing on a crucial Vīraśaiva text, the *Śūnyasampādane*, which explores the variety of forms and practices that characterize contemporary Vīraśaiva sectarian and denominational patterns. *Speaking of Basava* (1992), by K. Ishwaran, records the achievements of Basava, who waged a crusade against socio-cultural inequalities and economic-political subordination of the masses. He evaluates the religious culture of Lingāyatism in a comparative context and argues that it is not an offshoot of Hinduism, but a new religion that also distinguishes itself from a Bhakti religion.

Muffled Voices by S. B. Shintri et al. (1994) includes translations of selected "sayings" of some of the twelfth-century Vīraśaiva saints. M. Sivamurthy (1994) provides a translation of a philosophical work (*Paramānubhava bodhe*) of Sri Nijaguna Sivayogi, the sixteenth-century Vīraśaiva saint-poet. Now scholars have access to most of the Vīraśaiva classics in the English language. *Veerashaivism in India* (Ghugare, 1995) focuses on the origin and evolution of Viraśaivism in the subcontinent of India. This study describes the systems of philosophy and religion, socioeconomic and political life, and problems facing the community. A recent publication, *In Search of Śiva* (Ullagaddi, 1995), aims at the North American Vīraśaiva adolescents, adults of all ages, and the general public. It provides a history of the twelfth-century Vīraśaiva movement, the doctrines of Vīraśavism, and a description of the present-day Lingāyats.

It is too early to project the trends of Lingāyat research for the twenty-first century. However, we can hope, with reasonable certainty, that the recent trends manifested in the 1990s will not only continue, but also that new and innovative sociological researches on contemporary Lingāyat community structure and dynamics may emerge in the next century.

The foregoing analysis reveals at least three broad stages or phases of Vīraśaiva research traditions. The first phase, which commenced during the early nineteenth century and continued until the first decade of the twentieth century, is composed of a large majority of Western scholars. These observers from the west, based on very limited or no knowledge of the original sources, acquired only a fragmentary view of the Vīraśaiva religion and culture. With a few exceptions, they presented sketchy, descriptive, distorted, and misleading accounts of the Vīraśaiva religion and society.

The second phase of Vīras'aiva studies, which emerged in the 1920s, encompassed two streams of indigenous scholars. Based upon an extensive exploration and analysis of Vīraśaiva classics in Kannada and Sanskrit, they contributed a great deal to the growth of Vīraśaivism as one of the significant branches of knowledge. Their knowledge of the original sources, modern outlook, and experience as members of the community helped them provide an authentic and fairly reliable analysis of the Vīraśaiva religion and philosophy. However, some of these studies needed objective scientific scrutiny.

The third phase of Vīraśaiva research, undertaken since the 1960s, may be characterized as a distinct evolutionary process wherein most research and writing has occured predominantly in institutional settings such as universities and research institutes. Modern library facilities, research grants, university chairs, and foundations' support for publication have made the research process relatively less problematic for academics to engage in large-scale long-term research projects on the Vīraśaiva religion and culture.

Contemporary Vīraśaiva research has become more interdisciplinary in nature, compared to the second phase. Today, various disciplines in the humanities and social sciences have been focusing on the Vīraśaiva history, literature, religion, philosophy, society, and culture. The field of Vīraśaiva studies has evolved from its early stages of the lone researcher to that of the institutionally based researcher. Despite the efforts of a few sociologists during the past two decades, sociological research on the Vīraśaiva society and culture has not yet scratched the surface. A considerable segment of the publications on the Vīraśaiva religion, especially in the Kannada language, still seem to be panegyric and repetitive. They are primarily descriptive and more subjective, lacking critical analysis. A large number of studies, even now, happen to be on Basava and his reform movement. A majority of the authors are men. Women authors, and writings on women saints and their contributions, are limited. Almost everything written about the Lingāyats is written by them, often, it seems, with the non-Lingayat reader in mind. All of this is curious because, by and large, the study of Vīraśaivism is not only undertaken by Vīraśaivas, but is also read by them more than by any one else. A great proportion of the writing appears in journals that have been founded, edited, published, and subscribed to by Lingāyats. In almost all cases, both the editorial boards and the contributions to the journals are overwhelmingly Lingāyat, and most books are published by the Lingāyat religious and cultural organizations.

There is an implicit belief in the legitimacy of studying Lingāyatism. From this review it appears, with a few exceptions, that the Lingāyats have been more interested in studying Lingāyats than has anyone else. If, and when, in the future, probably in the mid-twenty-first century, someone else is asked to review the state of research on the Lingāyats, the literature may show signfiicantly different trends. At present, however, such a possibility seems remote. However, one can only hope that researches on the Lingāyat religion and culture in the twenty-first century will manifest the richness, diversity, and dynamics of the Lingāyat culture itself.

There is a need to formulate a new research agenda for the next millenium. It is necessary to reinterpret the Vīraśaiva classics and to demonstrate the relevance of the Lingāyat ideology of egalitarianism, the work ethic, nonviolence, and peace within the context of contemporary issues and problems. More social science research needs to be undertaken on contemporary Lingāyat cultural milieu and community issues regarding the changing roles of women, leadership patterns in the economy, politics, education, and, in other spheres, the role of Vīraśaiva monasteries, educational and philanthropic organizations, social stratification and mobility patterns, work and leisure, marriage, family, and community problems, children and youth, aging and intergenerational continuity and change, and the Lingāyat diaspora. These are a few among many facets that should be explored. Community-based micro-research, along with macro-cross-national longitudinal researches, would go a long way toward developing profiles of the mosaic of the contemporary Vīraśaiva society and culture.

Furthermore, the need to train a new generation of researchers cannot be ignored. The discipline would be enriched if the younger generation is provided with adequate facilities and incentives to undertake research on various aspects of the Vīraśaiva culture. A large pool of both indigenous, as well as foreign, scholars needs to be nurtured so that it is possible to have an insider's and an outsider's view of the subject of inquiry. Specifically for the purpose of encouraging scholarship in this field, courses in Vīraśaiva studies at the undergraduate and postgraduate levels, research and travel grants, fellowships, chairs and foundations, and so forth at different universities in India and abroad would go a long way toward developing this area as a viable academic discipline.

Needless to say, an increasing investment in the training of the next generation of researchers is important. Priority also should be given to developing and promoting research infrastructures that enhance the quality, productivity, and relevance of the research. It is necessary to ensure that the research results are more widely disseminated. Universities, research institutions, and research funding agencies should promote collaboration among researchers in the social sciences and humanities. International collaboration on macro-level long-term research projects could be emphasized. Research centers and research networks also may be utilized to meet the growing need for cost-effective collaborative research.

NOTES

Author's note: All brief quotations appearing in this book are author's translations from the original sources listed in the references.

1. Author's translation.
2. L. M. A. Menezes and S. M. Angadi, trans., *Vacanas of Basavanna*, ed. H. Deveerappa. Sirigere, India: Annana Balaga, 1967, p. 172.
3. V. C. Yagati, trans., *Vacanas or Gospels of Basava*, unpublished manuscript, 1950, p. 165.
4. Author's translation.
5. M. S. Sunkapur and L. M. A. Menezes, trans. and eds., *Śūnyasampādane*, vol. V. Dharwar, India: Karnatak University, 1972, p. 22.
6. S. C. Nandimath, L. M. A. Menezes, and R. C. Hiremath, trans. and eds., *Śūnyasampādane*, vol. I. Dharwar, India: Karnatak University, 1965, p. 56.
7. Author's translation.
8. Nandimath, Menezes, and Hiremath, *Śūnyasampādane*, vol. I. 1965, pp. 258-259.
9. S. S. Bhoosnurmath and L. M. A. Menezes, trans. and eds., *Śūnyasampādane*, vol. II. Dharwar, India: Karnatak University, 1968, p. 124.
10. Sunkapur and Menezes, *Śūnyasampādane*, vol. V. 1972, p. 336.
11. Yagati, 1950, p. 191.
12. Yagati, 1950, p. 192.
13. R. C. Hiremath, *Sri Channabasaveshvara: Life and Philosophy*. Dharwar, India: Karnatak University, 1978, p. 124.
14. S. S. Bhoosnurmath and L. M. A. Menezes, *Śūnyasampādane*, vol. III. Dharwar, India: Karnatak University, 1969, p. 320.
15. Hiremath, 1978, p. 77.
16. Bhoosnurmath and Menezes, *Śūnyasampādane*, vol. II. 1968, p. 49.
17. Sunkapur and Menezes, *Śūnyasampādane*, vol. V. 1972, p. 433.
18. Bhoosnurmath and Menezes, *Śūnyasampādane*, vol. III. 1969, p. 294.
19. Nandimath, Menezes, and Hiremath, *Śūnyasampādane*, vol. I. 1965, p. 81.
20. Nandimath, Menezes, and Hiremath, *Śūnyasampādane*, vol. I. 1965, p. 89.
21. Nandimath, Menezes, and Hiremath, *Śūnyasampādane*, vol. I. 1965, pp. 79-80.

22. Author's translation.
23. Author's translation.
24. Yagati, 1950, p. 15.
25. Bhoosnurmath and Menezes, *Śūnyasampādane,* vol. II. 1968, p. 171.
26. Yagati, 1950, p. 48.
27. Author's translation.
28. Yagati, 1950, p. 20.
29. Yagati, 1950, p. 162.
30. Menezes and Angadi, 1967, p. 81.
31. Yagati, 1950, p. 98.
32. Menezes and Angadi, 1967, p. 77.
33. Menezes and Angadi, 1967, p. 322.
34. Nandimath, Menezes, and Hiremath, *Śūnyasampādane,* vol. I. 1965, p. 116.
35. Author's translation.
36. Sunkapur and Menezes, *Śūnyasampādane,* vol. V. 1972, p. 341.
37. Yagati, 1950, p. 165.
38. Menezes and Angadi, 1967, p. 77.
39. Author's translation.
40. Author's translation.
41. Bhoosnurmath and Menezes, *Śūnyasampādane,* vol. II. 1968, p. 171.
42. Author's translation.
43. Hiremath, 1978, pp. 136-137.
44. Hiremath, 1978, p. 157.

GLOSSARY

Ādi-Śakti. Primeval energy/power.

Advaita. Monism, non-dualism.

Āgamas. Forms a part of the sacred books of the Hindus, ritual text.

Ahimsa. Nonviolence.

Aikya. Oneness or union with Lord Śiva; person who has attained Godhood.

Ānanda. Bliss.

Ānavamala. Impurities born of atoms.

Anga. The individual self or soul; śarana or devotee.

Anubhāva. Mystical experience.

Anubhava Mantapa. The Academy of Philosophy, a hall of spiritual experience located in Kalyāna where mystic discourses among the Vīraśaiva saints were held. The hall of experience of Śiva.

Aruhu. The divine consciousness.

Āsramas. The fourfold lifestages of traditional Hinduism.

Astāvarana. The eight aids, coverings, shields, or emblems.

Ātma. Soul, self.

Avidyā. Nescience, ignorance.

Bayalu. God, space, the absolute void; the universal soul of Śiva.

Bhakta. Devotee.

Bhakti. Devotion to a personal god; in Viraśaivism Bhakti refers to fervent and unconditional devotion to Śiva.

Bhāva. Will; self.

Bhāvalinga. Linga that is part of one's feeling or experience of the Lord; ultimate reality as inner ontos.

Bhogānga. The devotee enjoys along with Śiva.

Brahma. Forms a part of the trinity of Gods; God who is regarded as the creator of the universe.

Brahmarandra. The frontal brain.

Brityācāra. The socio-ethical code that emphasizes offering service to the poor and with the disadvantaged with modesty and humility.

Cārvākas. For whom there is no Self or entity beyond the material body and its needs. God and religion are illusion.

Cit. Intelligence; consciousness.

Citkala. The intellectual aspect of God; the supreme spark.

Dāsoha. Devoted service.

Dāsoham. Self surrender to God.

Desi. The populistic cultural traditions of India; also labeled as the Little Tradition.

Dīkśa. The ritual of purification or initiation into a spiritual life.

Dualism. Of God and soul.

Dwaita. Dualism of God and soul.

Ganācāra. The socio-ethical code that expects everyone to fight against injustice and immorality with courage and conviction.

Guru. Spiritual guide or master; preceptor; a manifestation of Śiva.

Hari. Forms a part of the trinity of Gods; God who is regarded as the protector of the universe.

Iccā-Śakti. Willpower.

Istalinga. Linga that is part of the individual self; Linga (a prototype symbol) worn on the body; the personal Linga given by the Guru at the time of initiation of the aspirant; ultimate reality as personal philactery; the personal divinity (linga), the symbol (Kuruhu) of the absolute worshipped by the Lingāyat.

Jangama. Itinerant religious mentor; the moving God — the Jangamalinga — free from desire or greed; priest; a manifestation of Śiva.

Jiva. Soul or the individual self.

Jivātma. The individual self or soul.

Jnānakānda. That segment of the Vedas dealing with knowledge.

Jnāna-śakti. Power of knowledge.

Jnānendriyas. The sense organs.

Kaivalya. Complete absorptions in God or final beatitude.

Kaliyuga. The fourth age of the aeon.

Kanāda. Philosopher of the Vaiśesika school of Hinduism.

Karma. The effect of former deeds, performed either in this life or in a previous one, on one's present and future condition.

Karmakānda. That segment of the Vedas dealing with karma or deeds.

Karmayoga. Yoga that concentrates on action as the basis for salvation.

Kārmika mala. Impurities born of action.

Kāyaka. Selfless work done in a spirit of dedication to God; bodily labor.

Kriyāśakti. Power of action.

Kuruhu. The symbol of Lord Śiva in the form of Istalinga.

Linga. Symbol of the God Śiva; Śiva representing the universe; a manifestation of Śiva as the supreme reality; universal soul.

Lingācāra. The socio-ethical code of conduct calling for strict devotion to Lord Śiva only and to be worshipped in the form of Istalinga.

Lingāyata. One who wears a Linga (a prototype symbol of God Śiva); the popular name for the Vīraśaivas and their community.

Mahālinga. The Great Linga, which is an undivided, all-pervasive, circular-shaped mass of light; ultimate reality.

Mahesha. Master of discipline.

Mantra. Sacred formula believed to have religious efficacy; "the Great Sacred Formula of Five Syllables" used by a devout Viraśaiva; prayers.

Mārga. The elitist cultural traditions of India; also labeled as the Great Tradition.

Matha. A Vīraśaiva monastery.

Māyā. Cosmic illusion; unreal; part of primeval energy (śakti).

Māyāmala. Impurities born of illusion.

Mimāmsa. One of the six Hindu philosophical systems.

Mukti. Liberation of the soul; Moksa — spiritual freedom.

Niranjanalinga. God without attributes.

Niśkala. God who is transcendent and formless.

Niśkalalinga. Formless God; absolute reality as partless.

Nivrtti. Disengagement.

Nyāya. One of the six Hindu philosophical systems.

Pādodaka. Holy water.

Pancācāra. The five socio-ethical codes of conduct.

Paramātma. God Śiva.

Parā-Śakti. Supreme power.

Pascimacakra. The hind part of the brain.

Pindajna. Fully awakened soul.

Prakrti. The primeval matter, nature, object.

Prāna. Life-breath.

Prānalinga. Linga that becomes part of one's life or heart; ultimate reality as inner breath.

Prānalingi. The phase of experiencing the Linga in the life-breath.

Prasāda. Consecrated food or grace.

Prasādi. A devotee who accepts pleasure and pain as God's gifts; acts as directed by God-inspired conscience and has no rebirth; receiving the Lord's grace.

Pravrtti. Engagement.

Purānas. Collections of stories and legends about the Hindu pantheon.

Puruśa. The primeval man, the person or the soul, subject, self or spirit.

Raja or Rajas. Passion.

Rudra. A manifestation of Śiva.

Rudrāksi. Rosary; prayer beads.

Sadācāra. The socio-ethical code of conduct that demands virtuous behavior, selfless work, and sharing.

Sādakhya. Eternal, indivisible, and imperceptible Light.

Sakala. God who is immanent and manifold.

Śakti. The Primeval energy or the supreme energy or power.

Śaktivisistādwaita. The divine-energy-qualified-monism or the philosophical position of Vīraśaivism.

Sālokya. Reaching heaven.

Sāmipya. Reaching the proximity of God.

Sampādane. Attainment (of God).

Sānkhya. One of the six schools of philosophy of Hinduism.

Śarana. The devotee who has surrendered to God; a saint; the surrendered; bliss; a devotee whose life is wholly lived in the divine; Vīraśaiva spiritual adept.

Sārupya. Assuming a similar form of God.

Sat. Existence or reality.

Śatsthala. The six-phase system of spiritual progress.

Satwa or Sātwika. Goodness; serenity.

Sāyujya. Entering into divine personality.

Śikhācakra. Central part of the brain.

Śiva. The supreme soul in the form of Śiva or Linga; the supreme deity of the Vīraśaivas.

Śivācāra. The Socio-ethical code that preaches social equality and religious democracy among the devotees of Śiva.

Śivāgamas. Holy scriptures of the Śiva tradition.

Śivayoga. A unique form of yoga contemplating and concentrating exclusively on Lord Śiva for attaining ultimate merger in Śiva.

Śūnya. The absolute void representing the universal soul of Śiva; the supreme reality.

Śūnya-Linga. The absolute void, God without name.

Sūtakas. Impurities.

Sthala. The absolute Linga, Śiva; the spiritual stage.

Tama or Tamas. Evil.

Tyāgānga. Renunciation of the world as transient.

Vacana. Sayings of the Vīraśaiva saints; these devotional lyrics are in poetic-prose (free-verse).

Vaiśesika. One of the six classical philosophical systems of Hinduism.

Varna. Caste-based system characteristic of Hindus.

Vedānta. One of the six classical philosophical systems of Hinduism.

Vedas. The sacred book of the Hindus containing hymns.

Vibhuti. Holy ash.

Virakta. Vīraśaiva monastic tradition in which celibacy is obligatory.

Vīraśaiva. One who is heroic (Veera) Śaiva; one who is a staunch devotee of Śiva and a strong defender of one's faith.

Vishnu. Forms a part of the trinity of gods; God who is regarded as the protector of the universe.

Visistādwaita. Qualifed monism.

Yoga. Mystical training or spiritual exercise; ascetic discipline; one of the six classical Hindu philosophical systems.

Yogānga. The devotee obtains happiness by his/her union with Śiva.

REFERENCES

Aerthayil, J. 1989. "Viraśaivism — A Śaivite Revolution in Karnataka." *Journal of Dharma* Vol. XIV.

Allchin, R. 1971. "The Attaining of the Void — A Review of Some Recent Contributions in English to the Study of Viraśaivism." *Religious Studies* Vol. 7.

Amur, G. S. and S. H. Ritti. 1968. *A Brief Lifesketch of Mrityunjaya Swamiji*. Dharwar, India: Shri Murughamath.

Ananthanarayana, S. (Trans.). 1988. *Thus Sang the Veerashaiva Mystics*, Vol. 1. *Allama Prabhu*. Vol. II. *Basavanna;* Vol. III. *Akkamahadevī*. Hubli, India: Moorusavirmath.

Arnold, D. et al. 1976. "Caste Associations in South India: A Comparative Analysis." *The Indian Economic & Social History Review* Vol. XIII.

Artal, R. C. 1909. "A Short Account of the Reformed Shaiva or Veerashaiva Faith." *Journal of the Anthropological Society of Bombay* Vol. III: No. 3.

Bagi, C. S. (Trans.). 1952. *Selected Sayings of Basava*. Belgaum, India: Vachana Mantapa.

Bali, A. P. 1979. "Organization of the Viraśaiva Movement: An Analysis in the Sect-Church Framework." In *Social Movements in India, II*, edited by M. S. A. Rao. New Delhi: Manohar.

Barnett, L. D. 1908. *The Heart of India: Sketches in the History of Hindu Religion and Morals*. London: J. Murray.

Barth, A. 1882. *Religions of India*. London: Trubner.

Basavanal, S. S. and K. R. S. Iyengar. (Trans.). 1941. *Musings of Basava*. Dharwar, India: Literary Committee, Lingāyat Education Association.

Basavaraju, L. (Trans.). 1969. *Allama's Vachanas*. Mysore, India: Geetha Book House.

Basham, A. L. 1954. *The Wonder That Was India*. London: Sidgwick and Jackson.

Bhandarkar, R. G. 1896. *Early History of the Dekkan*. (Reprint, 1957), Calcutta, India: Susil Gupta.

——. 1913. *Vaishnavism, Śaivism, and Minor Religious Systems*. Straussburg, Germany: K. J. Trubner.

Bhoosnurmath, S. S. 1979. *Man the Divine: A Critical Exposition of Shoonyasampādane*. Adoni, India: Mandagiri Kalmath.

Bhoosnurmath, S. S. and L. M. A. Menezes. (Trans. and Eds.). 1968. *Śūnyasampādane* Vol. II. Dharwar, India: Karnatak University.

Bhoosnurmath, S. S. and L. M. A. Menezes. (Trans. and Eds.). 1969. *Śūnyasampādane* Vol. III. Dharwar, India: Karnatak University.

Bhoosnurmath, S. S. and L. M. A. Menezes. 1970. *Śūnyasampādane* Vol. IV. Dharwar, India: Karnatak University.

Bradford, N. J. 1985. "The Indian Renouncer: Structure and Transformation in the Lingāyat Community." In *Indian Religion*, edited by R. Burghart and A. Cantlie. London/New York: Curzon Press/St. Martin's Press.

Brown, C. P. 1840a. "Account of the Basava Puran: The Principal Book Used as a Religious Code by the Jangams." *Madras Journal of Literature and Science* Vol. XI.

——. 1840b. "Essay on the Creed, Customs, and Literature of the Jangams." *Madras Journal of Literature and Science, Series I* Vol. II: No. 26.

Buchanan, F. 1811. *Journey from Madras through the Countries of Mysore, Canara, and Malabar, 1800-1801.* London: Longman.

Bucky, P. A. 1992. *The Private Albert Einstein.* Kansas City, Mo: Andrews and McMeel.

Campbell, J. 1918. "Basava: A Social Reformer." *Times of India.* (April 17).

Carr, R. C. 1906. *Monograph on Lingāyats.* Madras, India: Government Press.

Chakravarti, R. 1957. *Śaktivisistādwaita or the Philosophical Aspect of Viraśaivism.* Mysore, India: Sri Panchacharya Electric Press.

Chamke, B. M. 1990. *Mystic Vision of Veerashaivism.* Latur, India: Author.

Channabasavappa, B. 1971. *Yediyur Siddhalingeshwara Swamy: Brief Life Sketch.* Bangalore, India: Fifth Centenary Celebration Committee.

Chekki, D. A. 1968. "Mate Selection, Age at Marriage and Propinquity Among the Lingāyats of India." *Journal of Marriage and the Family* Vol. 30: No. 4.

——. 1969. "Social Legislation and Kinship in India," *Journal of Marriage and the Family* Vol. 31: No. 3.

——. 1974. *Modernization and Kin Network.* Leiden, The Netherlands: E. J. Brill

——. (Trans.). 1986. *Guru Bless Me With Your Grace.* Scarborough, Canada: Veerashaiva Samaja of North America.

Chitnis, K. N. 1967. "Viraśaiva Mathas in the Keladi Kingdom." *Journal of the Karnatak University (Social Sciences)* Vol. III.

Christianson, G. E. 1984. *In the Presence of the Creator: Isaac Newton and His Times.* New York: The Free Press.

Dasgupta, Surendranath. 1955. "Viraśaivism." In *A History of Indian Philosophy* Vol. V. Cambridge: Cambridge University Press.

Desai, P. B. 1968. *Basaveshwara and His Times.* Dharwar, India: Karnatak University.

Doddamani, G.S. 1997. *Veerashaiva Samaja of North America, Directory.* Detroit, MI: Veerashaiva Samaja of North America.

Dubois, J. A. 1908. *Hindu Manners, Customs and Ceremonies.* Oxford: Clarendon Press.

Durkheim, E. 1995. *The Elementary Forms of Religious Life,* translated by K. E. Fields. New York: The Free Press.

Einstein, A. 1973. *Ideas and Opinions.* New York: Dell.

Embree, A. T. (Ed.). 1966. *The Hindu Tradition.* New York: Vintage.

Enthoven, R. E. 1915. "Lingāyats." In *Encyclopaedia of Religion and Ethics* Vol. VIII, edited by James Hastings. New York: Charles Scribner's.

——. 1923. *The Tribes and Castes of Bombay* Vol. II. Bombay, India: Government Central Press.

Farquhar, J. N. 1915. *Modern Religious Movements in India.* New York: MacMillan.

——. 1925. *An Outline of the Religious Literature of India.* London: Oxford University Press.

Fleet, J. F. 1899. "Ablur Inscriptions." *Epigraphia Indica* Vol. 5.

Geertz, C. 1973. *The Interpretation of Cultures.* New York: Basic Books.

Ghugare, S. B. 1995. *Veerashaivism in India.* Gadhinglaj, India: Sadhana.

Goode, W. 1963. *World Revolution and Family Patterns.* New York: The Free Press.

Gordon, M. M. 1964. *Assimilation in American Life.* New York: Oxford University Press.

Gunjal, S. R. 1989. *Lingāyat Bibliography: A Comprehensive Sourcebook.* Bhalki, India: Basava Dharma Prachara Samsthe Hiremath.

Hadimani, R. N. 1988. "The Protestant Ethic in Basava's Teachings." *Basava Journal* Vol. 13: 1-2.

Hardekar, M. (Ed.). 1939. *Social Structure of the Vīraśaiva Saints.* Dharwar, India: Lingaraja Art Press.

Hassan, S. S. U. 1920. *The Castes and Tribes of H.E.H. The Nizam's Dominions.* Vol. I. Bombay, India: The Times Press.

Hill, R. and P. Shankara (Trans.). 1983. *Naming the Nameless: 101 Vachanas.* Mysore, India: Nivedita Prakashana.

Hiremath, L. G. 1972. *Shri Kumar Shivayogi of Hangal.* Hubli, India: Moorusaviramatha.

Hiremath, R. C. 1978. *Sri Channabasaveshvara: Life and Philosophy.* Dharwar, India: Karnatak University.

Hulbanni, S. 1990. "President's Message." *Veerashaiva* Vol. 13 (December).

Hunshal, S. M. 1947. *The Lingāyat Movement: A Social Revolution in Karnatak.* Dharwar, India: Karnatak Sahitya Mandira.

———. 1957. *The Veerashaiva Social Philosophy.* Raichur, India: Amaravani Printing Press.

Hutton, J. H. 1946. *Caste in India.* Cambridge: Cambridge University Press.

Ishwaran, K. 1966. *Tradition and Economy in Village India.* London: Routledge and Kegan Paul.

———. 1968. *Shivapur: A South Indian Village.* London: Routledge and Kegan Paul.

———. 1977. *A Populistic Community and Modernization in India.* Leiden, The Netherlands: E. J. Brill.

———. 1983. *Religion and Society Among the Lingāyats of South India.* Leiden, The Netherlands: E. J. Brill.

———. 1992. *Speaking of Basava.* Boulder, CO: Westview Press.

Iyengar, M.V. 1935. *Sayings of Basavanna.* Gadag, India: Veerashaiva Taruna Sangha.

Iyer, L. K. A. K. 1931. *The Mysore Tribes and Castes* Vol. IV, Mysore, India: University of Mysore.

Jangam, R. T. 1985. "Basaveshwara and the Ideal of Social Equality." *Basava Journal* Vol. IX: No. 3.

Kambi, V. S. 1973. *Philosophy of the Śūnyasampādane,* 2 Vols. Dharwar, India: Kumaresh.

Karmarkar, A. P. 1950. *The Religions of India.* Lonavala, India. Mira Publishing House.

Kittel, Rev. F. 1875a. "Old Kanarese Literature: Lingaita Literature." *Indian Antiquary* Vol. IV.

———. 1875b. "Seven Lingāyata Legends." *Indian Antiquary* Vol. IV.

Krishnarao, M. V. 1959. *The Mystic Tradition.* Madras, India: Wardha.

Kumaraswamiji. 1941. *Veerashaiva Weltanschauung.* Dharawar, India: Navakalyana Matha.

———. 1952. "Vira-Saivism." In *History of Philosophy: Eastern and Western* Vol. I, edited by S. Radhakrishnan. London: George Allen & Unwin.

———. 1960a. *Mirror of Vīraśaivism.* Dharwar, India: Navakalyana Matha.

———. 1960b. *The Virashaiva Philosophy and Mysticism.* Dharwar, India: Navakalyana Matha.

Kumbar, U. N. 1982. "Demographic and Geographic Study of Veerashaiva Families in North America." *Veerashaiva* Vol. IV: No. 1.

Kumagai, F. 1986. "Modernization and the Family in Japan." *Journal of Family History* Vol.

11: No. 4.

Lipset, S. M. 1959. "American Intellectuals: Their Politics and Status." *Daedalus* (Summer).

Lorenzen, D. 1972. *Kapalikas and Kalamukhas: Two Lost Saivite Sects.* Berkeley, CA: University of California Press.

Mackenzie, J. S. 1924. *A Manual of Ethics.* London: University Tutorial Press.

Macnicol, N. 1915. *Indian Theism.* London: Oxford University Press.

Mahant, R. 1989. "To Be or Not to Be a Lingāyat; That Is the Question." *Voice of a New Generation.* (August).

Mandelbaum, D. G. 1970. *Society in India.* Berkeley, CA: University of California Press.

Manuel, F. E. 1974. *The Religion of Isaac Newton.* Oxford: Clarendon Press.

Marro, C. 1974. "Role and Position of the Guru and the Jangam in Lingāyatism." *Bangalore Theological Forum* Vol. 6: No. 2.

Mate, Mahadevi. 1986. *Lingāyatism.* Bangalore, India: Viswakalyana Mission.

Menezes, L. M. A. 1971. *Songs From the Śaranas and Other Poems.* Dharwar, India: Karnatak University.

———. 1976. "Basavanna: Mystic and Poet." *Journal of the Karnatak University (Humanities)* Vol. XX.

Menezes, L. M. A.; and S. M. Angadi, (Trans.). 1967. *Vacanas of Basavanna,* edited by H. Deveerappa. Sirigere, India: Annana Balaga.

———. 1973. *Vacanas of Akkamahādevi.* Dharwar, India: M. A. Adke.

———. 1978. *Essence of Śatsthala: Vacanas of Tontada Siddhalingeśvara.* Dharwar, India: Karnatak University.

McCormack, W. 1959. "The Forms of Communication in Vīraśaiva Religion." In *Traditional India: Structure and Change,* edited by M. Singer. Philadelphia, PA: American Folklore Society.

———. 1963. "Lingāyats as a Sect." *Journal of the Royal Anthropological Institute* Vol. 93.

———. 1973. "On Lingāyat Culture." In *Speaking of Śiva,* translated by A. K. Ramanujan. Harmondsworth, U.K.: Penguin Books.

Michael, R. B. 1982. "Linga as Lord Supreme in the Vacanas of Basava." *Numen* 29: 2.

———. 1983a. "Foundation Myths of the Two Denominations of Viraśaivism: Viraktas and Gurusthalins." *Journal of Asian Studies* XLII: 2.

———. 1983b. "Work as Worship in Viraśaiva Tradition." *Journal of the American Academy of Religion* 50: 4.

———. 1983c. "Women of the Śūnyasampādane: Housewives and Saints in Vīraśaivism." *Journal of the American Oriental Society* 103: 2.

———. 1990. "Laicization of the Ascetic Ideal: The Case of the Viraśaivas." In *Monastic Life in the Christian and Hindu Traditions,* edited by A. B. Creed and V. Narayanan. Lewiston, NY: Edwin Mellen Press.

———. 1992. *The Origins of Vīraśaiva Sects.* Delhi, India: Motilal.

Mill, J. S. 1970. *The Subjection of Women.* New York: Sourcebook Press.

Miller, D. 1976-77. "The Guru as the Centre of Sacredness." *Studies in Religion* (Summer).

More, L. T. 1934. *Issac Newton: A Biography.* New York: Dover.

Mullatti, L. 1989. *The Bhakti Movement and the Status of Women: A Case Study of Vīraśaivism.* New Delhi, India: Manohar.

Murthy, M. C. 1972. *Basavanna.* New Delhi, India: National Book Trust.

Naikar, B. (Trans.). 1990. *Musings of Sarvajna.* Dharwar, India: Sivaranjani Publications.

Nandi, R. N. 1975. "Origin of the Vīraśaiva Movement." *Indian Historical Review* 2: 1.

Nandimath, S. C. 1962. "Śaivāgamas: Their Literature and Theology." *Journal of the Karnatak University (Humanities)* Vol. 6.

———. 1964. "Sri Basaveśvara." *Journal of the Karnatak University (Humanitics)* Vol. 8.

———. 1979. *A Handbook of Vīraśaivism* (First edition 1942), Second edition revised and edited by R. N. Nandi. Delhi, India: Motilal.

Nandimath, S. C., L. M. A. Menezes, and R. C. Hiremath. (Trans. and Eds.). 1965. *Śūnyasampādane* Vol. I, Dharwar, India: Karnatak University.

Narayana Rao, V. and G. H. Roghair (Trans.). 1990. *Śiva's Warriors: The Basava Purana of Palkurike Somanatha*. Princeton, NJ: Princeton University Press.

O'Malley, L. 1935. *Popular Hinduism*. New York: Macmillan.

Oren, S. 1973. "Killing a Myth: A Note on the Lingāyat Mutts of Mysore State and Their Political Influence." *Journal of Indian History* (Golden Jubilee Volume).

Padoux, A. 1987. "Saivism: An Overview." In *The Encyclopaedia of Religion*, Vol. 13, edited by Mircea Eliade. New York: Macmillan.

Paraddi, M. 1976. "Viraśaivism in Sanskrit Literature." *Journal of the Karnatak University (Humanities)* Vol. XX.

Parsons, T. 1958. "The Kinship System of the Contemporary United States." In *Essays in Sociological Theory: Pure and Applied*. Glencoe, IL: The Free Press.

Parvathamma, C. 1971. *Politics and Religion*. New Delhi, India: Sterling.

———. 1972. *Sociological Essays on Veerashaivism*. Bombay, India: Popular.

———. 1978. "Religion and Social Change: A Study of Tradition and Change in Viraśaivism." In *Dimensions of Social Change in India*, edited by M. N. Srinivas, et al. Columbia, MO: South Asia Books.

Patil, B. A. 1975. *Akka Mahādevi: The Divine Cuckoo*. Gulbarga, India: Siddhavageesha Prakashana.

Pawate, S. D. 1927. *Viraśaiva Philosophy of the Śaivāgamas*. Hubli, India: (Publisher unknown).

Puranik, S. 1986. *Mahādevi*, translated by G. B. Sajjan. Dharwar, India: Karnatak University.

Puttanna Chetty, K. P. 1917. *Presidential Address at the All-India Veerashaiva Conference*. December 27. Davangeri, India: (Publisher unknown).

Radhakrishnan, S. 1927. *Indian Philosophy* Vol. 2. London: George Allen and Unwin.

Radhakrishnan, S. and C. A. Moore (Eds.). 1967. *A Sourcebook in Indian Philosophy*. Princeton, NJ.: Princeton University Press.

Ramanujan, A. K. (Trans.). 1973. *Speaking of Śiva*. Harmondsworth, UK: Penguin Books.

Renou, L. (Ed.). 1963. *Hinduism*. New York: Washington Square Press.

Rice, B. L. 1886. *Mysore and Coorg: A Gazetteer*. Bangalore, India: Mysore Government Press.

———. 1909. *Mysore and Coorg from the Inscriptions*. London: Constable.

Rice, E. P. 1921. *A History of Kannada Literature*. (Reprint, 1982), New Delhi, India: Asian Educational Service.

Risley, H. H. 1908. *The People of India*. London: W. Thacker.

Sadasivaiah, H. M. 1967. *A Comparative Study of Two Viraśaiva Monasteries*. Mysore, India: University of Mysore.

Sakhare, M. R. 1978. *History and Philosophy of Lingāyat Religion* (First edition, 1942). Dharwar, India: Karnatak University.

Samartha, M. P. 1977. "Basava's Spiritual Struggle." *Religious Studies* Vol. 13.

Sargant, N. C. 1963. *The Lingāyats: The Viraśaiva Religion*. Bangalore, India: Christian Institute for the Study of Religion and Society.

Scharf, B. R. 1971. *The Sociological Study of Religion*. New York: Harper Torchbooks.

Schouten, J. P. 1991. *Revolution of the Mystics: On the Social Aspects of Viraśaivism*. Kampen, The Netherlands: KokPharos.

Seshagiri Rao, D. (Trans.). 1981. *At the Lord's Feet: Selected Vachanas of Akka Mahādevi*. Bangalore, India: Parijat Publications.

Shastri, K. A. N. 1958. *A History of South India*. Madras, India: Oxford University Press.

Shintri, S. B. 1984. "Women in the Vīraśaiva Movement." *Basava Journal*, Vol. 8: No. 4.

Shintri, S. B. et al. (Trans.). 1994. *Muffled Voices (Translations of Selected Vacanas)*. Sirigere, India: Sri Taralabalu Jagadguru Brihanmath.

Shivarudrappa, G. 1975. "Contributions of Veerashaiva Mathas to the Development of Education in Karnatak from 12th to 18th Century A.D." *Journal of the Karnatak University (Social Sciences)* Vol. XI.

Singer, M. 1972. *When a Great Tradition Modernizes*. New York: Praeger.

Sivamurthy, M. (Trans.). 1994. *Sri Nijaguna Sivayogi's Paramanubhava Bodhe*. Bombay, India: Bharatiya Vidya Bhavan.

Steele, A. H. 1868. *The Law and Customs of Hindu Castes*. London: W. H. Allen.

Sunkapur, M. S. and L. M. A. Menezes. (Trans. and Eds.). 1972. *Śūnyasampādane* Vol. V. Dharwar, India: Karnatak University.

Thapar, R. 1996. *History of India*. New York: Penguin.

Theodore, A. S. & Hakari, D. (Trans.). 1965. *Thus Spake Basava*. Bangalore, India: Basava Samiti.

Thipperudraswamy, H. 1968. *The Viraśaiva Saints: A Study*. Mysore, India: Rao & Raghavan.

———. 1975. *Basaveshwara*. Delhi, India: Sahitya Academy.

———. 1982. *Soul Unto the Sublime: Novel on th Life of Akka Mahādevi*, translated by C. N. Hiremath. Hubli, India: Murusavira Math.

———. 1983. *The Light That Never Was: Novel on the Life of Nijaguna Sivayogi*, translated by C. N. Hiremath. Hubli, India: Murusaviramath.

———. 1985. *Towards Perfection: Novel on the Life of Allamaprabhu*, translated by C. N. Hiremath. Hubli: India, Murusavirarmath.

Thurston, E. 1909. *Castes and Tribes of Southern India* Vol. IV. Madras, India: Government Press.

Tönnies, F. 1957. *Community and Society: Gemeinschaft und Gessellschaft*, translated and edited by C. P. Loomis. New York: Harper.

Ullagaddi, S. 1995. *In Search of Śiva*. Dublin, OH: Veerashaiva Samaja of North America.

Uplaonkar, A. T. 1990. "Occupational Patterns of Viraśaiva and Non-Viraśaiva College Students." *Basava Journal*, Vol. 14: No. 4.

Uttangi, C. D. 1955. *Anubhava Mantapa: The Heart of Lingāyat Religion*. (Reprint 1982), edited by S. R. Gunjal. Dharwar, India: Uttangi Centenary Commemoration Committee.

Veerashaiva. 1986. *Veerashaiva Samaja of North America, Directory*. *Veerashaiva*, Vol. 8: No. 2.

———. 1995. *Veerashaiva Samaja of North America, Directory*. *Veerashaiva*, Vol. 18: No. 1.

Venugopal, C. N. 1977. "Factor of Antipollution in the Ideology of Lingāyat Movement." *Sociological Bulletin* Vol. 26: No. 2.

———. 1980. "Some Aspects of Lingāyat Ideology and Monastic Organization." *Eastern Anthropologist* Vol. 33: No. 4.

———. 1982. "Lingayat Ideology of Salvation: An Enquiry into Some of Its Social Dimensions." *Religion and Society* Vol. XXIX: No.4.

Weber, M. 1968. *The Religion of India*, translated and edited by Hans H. Gerth and Don Martindale. New York: The Free Press.

Wilks, M. 1980. *Historical Sketches of the South Indian History* (First edition, 1810). New Delhi, India: Cosmo.

Williams, M. 1883. *Religious Thought and Life in India*. London: John Murray.

Wilson, H. H. 1828-1832. *"Religious Sects of the Hindus."* *Asiatic Researches* Vol. XVI and Vol. XVII.

Wirth, L. 1938. *"*Urbanism as a Way of Life."* *American Journal of Sociology,* Vol. 44: No. 2.

Wodeyar, S. S. (Ed.). 1967. *Sri Basaveshwara: Eighth Centenary Commemoration Volume.* Bangalore, India: Government of Mysore.

——. 1975. *Basaveshwara: The Great Emancipator.* Hubli, India: Gurudev Literary Association.

Wolf, H. C. 1978. "The Linga as Center: A Study in Religious Phenomonolgy." *Journal of the American Academy of Religion* Vol. XLVI : No. 3.

Wollstonecraft, M. 1975. *A Vindication of the Rights of Women,* edited by C. Poston. New York: Norton.

Wurth, Rev. G. (Trans.). 1864-65. "Channa Basava Purana of the Lingaits." *Journal of the Royal Asiatic Society* (Bombay Branch) Vol. VIII: No. XXIV.

——. 1868. "The Basava Purana of the Lingaits." *Journal of the Royal Asiatic Society* (Bombay Branch) Vol. VIII: No. XXIV.

Yagati, V. C. 1928. "Basava: The Reviver of Lingāyatism." *The Indian Social Reformer.* (April 7).

——. 1942. "Basaveswara Vachana." *Journal of the Literary Committee of the L. E. Association* Vol. 2.

——. 1943. "Veerashaivism." *Journal of the Literary Committee of the L. E. Association* Vol. 2: No. 4.

——. 1943-1946. "Shoonyasampādane or the Attainment of God." *Journal of the Literary Committee of the L. E. Association* Vols. II-V.

——. 1947. "Veerashaiva Culture." *Journal of the Literary Committee of the L. E. Association* Vol. VII: Nos. 1-2.

——. 1950. (Trans.). *Vacanas or Gospels of Basava,* unpublished manuscript.

——. 1985-1988. "Shoonyasampādane or the Attainment of God." *Basava Journal* Vols. IX-XII.

Yaravintelimath, C. R. 1976. "Muktāyakka." *Journal of the Karnatak University (Humanities)* Vol. XX.

——. 1987. *The Caste Eradication Vacanas of Shri Basaveśwara.* Dharwar, India: Karnatak University.

Zvelebil, K. V. (Trans.). 1984. *The Lord of the Meeting Rivers: Devotional Poems of Basavanna.* Delhi, India: Motilal/Paris: UNESCO.

WORKS IN KANNADA

Akhandeśvara Vacanagalu of Shanmukhaswami. 1944. Edited by Siddhaviradevaru. Dharwad, India: Murugha Matha.

Allama prabhudevara vacana Samputa. 1993. Vol. 2, edited by B. V. Mallapur. Bangalore, India: Government of Karnatak, Department of Kannada and Culture.

Allaman Vacana Candrike. 1986. Edited by L. Basavaraju. Hubli, India: Murusavira Matha.

Allama Prabhudevara vacanagalu. 1976. Edited by R. C. Hiremath and M. S. Sunkapur. Dharwad, India: Karnatak University.

Anubhava Mantapa. 1971. By H. Thipperudraswamy. Mysore, India: D. V. K. Murthy.

Basava Purāna (of Bhimakavi). 1971. Edited by R. C. Hiremath. Dharwad, India: Murugha Matha.

Basavannanavara Vacana samputa. 1993. Vol. 1, edited by M. M. Kalburgi. Bangalore, India: Government of Karnatak, Department of Kannada and Culture.

Basavannanavara Vacanagalu. 1962. Edited by S .S. Basavanal. Dharwad, India: Literary Committee, L. E. Association.

Basavannanavara Vacanagalu. 1968. Edited by R. C. Hiremath. Dharwad, India: Karnatak University.

Basavannanavarannu Kuritu Sāsanagalu. 1973. By M. M. Kalburgi. Dharwad, India: Karnatak University.

Basavarājavijayam (of Maha Kavi Sadakśaradeva). 1968. Edited by R. C. Hiremath. Dharwad: India: Karnatak University.

Bhakti Bhāndāri Basavannanavaru. 1931. By M. R. Srinivás Mūrti. Bangalore, India: Central College, Karnatak Sangha.

Cannabasavannanavara Vacanagalu. 1965. Edited by R. C. Hiremath. Dharwad, India: Karrnatak University.

Cennabasaveśvara Vacana Samputa. 1993. Vol. 3, edited by B. V. Mallapur. Bangalore, India: Government of Karnatak, Department of Kannada and Culture.

Basavarāja devara Ragale (of Harihara). 1976. Edited by T. S. Venkannayya. Mysore, India: T. S. Venkannayya smāraka granthamale.

Dēvara dāsimayyana Vacanagalu. 1966. Edited by P. G. Halakatti. Dharwad, India: Samaj Pustakalaya.

Hariharana Ragalegalu: Samgrasamputa. 1968. Edited by P. G. Halakatti (1930), Introduction by B. V. Mallapur (Reprint). Dharwad, India: Samaj Pustakalaya.

Ippatēlu Śivaśaraneyara Vacanagalu. 1968. Edited by R. C. Hiremath. Dharwad, India: Karnatak University.

Lingalilā vilāsa Caritra (of Kallumathada Prabhudeva). 1956. Edited by S. S. Bhoosnurmath. Dharwad, India: Murugha Matha.

Mahadeviyakkana Vacanagalu. 1973. Edited by R. C. Hiremath. Dharwad, India: Karnatak University.

Mailara Sri Basavalinga Śaranara Kritigalu (of Basavalinga Saranaru). 1962. Edited by S. S. Basavanal. Dharwad, India: Murugha Matha.

Mailāra Basavalinga Śaranara Gurukaruna Trividhiyalli Virasaiva Darśnika Siddhanta. 1989. Edited by Sri Annadāneeśvara Maha Swamigalu. Mundaragi, India: Sri Jagadguru Samsthana Matha.

Nilammana Vacanagalu mattu Lingammana Vacanagalu. 1971. Edited by R. C. Hiremath. Dharwad, India: Karnatak University.

Prabhulinga lile (of Cāmarasa). 1971. Edited by S. S. Basavanal. Dharwad, India: Literary Committee, L. E. Association (1938).

Sakala-purātanara Vacanagalu. 1972. Edited by R. C. Hiremath. Dharwad, India: Karnatak University.

Samāja, Dharma, Sanskruti. 1975. By V. C. Yagati. Dharwad, India: Vichara Vikas Prakashana.

Samkirana vacana samputa. 1993. Vol. 6, edited by M. M. Kalburgi. Bangalore, India: Government of Karnatak, Department of Kannada and Culture.

Samkirana vacana samputa. 1993. Vol. 7, edited by S. Vidyā Śankara. Bangalore, India: Government of Karnatak, Department of Kannada and Culture.

Samkirana vacana samputa. 1993. Vol. 8, edited by B. R. Hiremath. Bangalore, India: Government of Karnatak, Department of Kannada and Culture.

Samkirana vacana samputa. 1993. Vol. 9, edited by B. R. Hiremath. Bangalore, India: Government of Karnatak, Department of Kannada and Culture.

Samkirana vacana samputa. 1993. Vol. 10, edited by V. Rajur. Bangalore, India: Government of Karnatak, Department of Kannada and Culture.

Samkirana vacana samputa. 1993. Vol. 11, edited by S. Śivanna. Bangalore, India:

Government of Karnatak, Department of Kannada and Culture.

Samkirana vacana samputa. 1993. Vol. 12, edited by V. Rajur. Bangalore, India: Government of Karnatak, Department of Kannada and Culture.

Samkirana vacana samputa. 1993. Vol. 13, edited by V. Rajur. Bangalore, India: Government of Karnatak, Department of Kannada and Culture.

Samkirana vacana samputa. 1993. Vol. 14, edited by V. Rajur. Bangalore, India: Government of Karnatak, Department of Kannada and Culture.

Sarvajnana vacanagalu. 1990. Edited by L. Basavaraju. Mysore, India: Gita Book House.

Satsthala jñāna sārāmruta (of Sri Tōntada Siddhalinga Śivayogi). 1983. Edited by R. C. Hiremath. Gadag, India: Vīraśaiva Adhyana Samsthe.

Siddharāmesvara vacana samputa. 1993. Vol. 4, edited by S. Vidyā Śankara. Bangalore, India: Government of Karnatak, Department of Kannada and Culture.

Siddharāmesvara Vacanagahu. 1968. Edited by R. C. Hiremath. Dharwad: Karnatak University.

Siddharāma cāritra (of Rāghavānka). 1975. Edited by T. S. Venkannayya and D. L. Narasimhācār. Mysore, India: T. S. Venkannyya Smāraka granthamāle.

Śivaśaraneyara vacana samputa. 1993. Vol. 5, edited by V. Rajur. Bangalore, India: Government of Karnatak, Department of Kannada.

Śūnyasampādane (of Gūlūra Siddaviranaryaru). 1930. Edited by P. G. Halakatti. Bijapur, India: Editor.

Śūnyasampādane (of Gūlūra Siddhaviranāryaru). 1958. Edited by S. S. Bhoosnurmath, Advani, India: Kalmath.

Śūnyasampādane Vivaranatmaka Paricaya. 1973. By H. Thipperudraswamy. Mysore, India: D. V. K. Murthy.

Vacana dharma sāra. 1968. By M. R. Srinivās Mūrti. Mysore, India: Mysore University.

Vacana Paribhāśa Kośa. 1993. Vol. 15, edited by S. Vidya Śankara. Bangalor, India: Government of Karnatak, Department of Kannada and Culture.

Vacanagalalli Viraśaiva dharma. 1982. By H. Thipperudraswamy. Mysore: D. V. K. Murthy.

Vacana śāstra sāra. 1982. By P. G. Halakatti. Bijapur 1933; Part I, reprinted, edited by M. M. Kalburgi and V. B. Rajur. Dambal-Gadag, India: Viraśaiva Adhyana Samsthe.

Vacana śāstra Rahasya. 1968. By R. R. Diwakar, 4th edition. Hubli, India: Murusavira Matha.

Yagati Veerappanavaru. 1993. By S. R. Gunjal. Dambala-Gadag, India: Viraśaiva Adhyana Samsthe.

WORKS IN SANSKRIT

Lingadhāranachandrika of Nandikeshwara with translation and full notes. 1942. History and Philosophy of Lingāyat Religion, edited and translated by M. R. Sakhare. Belgaum, India: Author.

Siddhānta Śikhāmani (of Śivayōgi). 1972. Edited with a commentary by Pandita Kāsinātha Sāstri. Mysore, India: Sri Pancācārya Electric Press.

Śivāgama Sangrah. 1941. Edited and published by Pandita Kāsinātha Sāśtri. Mysore, India: Sri Pancācārya Electric Press.

Śivānubhava sūtram (of Sri Māyidēva). 1969. Edited by Y. Nagesa Sāstri. Dharwad, India: Murugha Math.

The Śrikara Bhāshya (of Śripati Pandita). 1936. Vīraśaiva Commentary on the Vedānta Sūtras. 2 vols, edited by C. Hayavadana Rao. Bangalore, India: No publisher.

INDEX

About the Author

DAN A. CHEKKI is Professor of Sociology at the University of Winnipeg. His books include *New Communities in a Changing World* (1996), *American Sociological Hegemony* (1987), and *Modernization and Kin Network* (1974).

ISBN 0-313-30251-0

EAN

90000>

9 780313 302510

HARDCOVER BAR CODE